Gravity Works

Written & Illustrated by
B. K. Hixson

> YOU KNOW, IF WE DID THIS ON THE MOON HE'D ONLY BREAK ONE-SIXTH THE BONES.

GravityWorks

Published by Loose in the Lab, Inc.
9462 South 560 West
Sandy, Utah 84070

www.looseinthelab.com

Library of Congress Cataloging-in-Publication Data:

Hixson, B. K.
    GravityWorks/B. K. Hixson
    p.   cm.-(Loose in the Lab Science Series)

    Includes glossary and index
    ISBN 0-9660965-4-1
    1. Flight and air pressure-experiments-juvenile lit-
erature. [1. Flight and air pressure-Experiments 2. Ex-
periments] I.B. K. Hixson IV. Loose in the Lab V. Title
VI. Series
QP441.D54   2001
152.14

Printed in the United States of America
Prop clear!

Dedication

Dr. Calvin Richardson

For my friend and inventor sans peer. Pictured above as a skinny eighteen-year-old greeting his friend Amelia Earhart on a visit to Salt Lake City many moons ago.

Thank you for all the conversations that provided new insights into flight, chemistry, and physics in general. You are truly a unique individual. Thank you for your support of all that we do and your ongoing love of kids, science, and education.

Many happy landings!

Bryce

Acknowledgments

Getting a book out for public consumption is far from a one-man job. There are lots of thank-yous to be doodled out and at the risk of leaving someone out, we attempt to do that on this page. In terms of my flying education, the top of the list is reserved for The Reverend Bob Carpenter, the father of one of my good friends and Alaskan bush pilot who uses his flying skills (sic) to bring unsuspecting tourists closer to God sooner than they expected. Meryl Mills, father of another good friend from college, who builds his own planes and entertains us with stories of trying to land on dirt roads with an extremely full set of kidneys. Bob Harney and Eldon Evans deserve a line for their creative use of U.S. Forest Service markers as navigational guides. And finally, Rick Littlefield, who took me on my most memorable flight in a small plane around Mt. Hood.

As for my educational outlook, the hands-on perspective, and the use of humor in the classroom, Dr. Fox, my senior professor at Oregon State University, gets the credit for shaping my educational philosophy while simultaneously recognizing that even at the collegiate level we were onto something a little different. He did his very best to encourage, nurture, and support me while I was getting basket loads of opposition for being willing to swim upstream. There were also several colleagues who helped to channel my enthusiasm during those early, formative years of teaching: Dick Bishop, Dick Hinton, Dee Strange, Connie Ridgway, and Linda Zimmermann. Thanks for your patience, friendship, and support.

Next up are all the folks that get to do the dirty work that make the final publication look so polished but very rarely get the credit they deserve. Our resident graphics guru Kris Barton gets a nod for scanning and cleaning the artwork you find on these pages, as well as putting together the graphics that make up the cover. A warm Yankee yahoo to Sue Moore our editor who passes her comments on so that Kathleen Hixson, Diane Burns, and Sue Moore (once again) can take turns simultaneously proofreading the text while mocking my writing skills.

Once we have a finished product, it has to be printed by the good folks at Advanced Graphics—Michael Williams, Matt and the crew—so that, Louisa Walker, Kent Walker, and the Delta Education gang can market and ship the books, collect the money, and send us a couple of nickels. It's a short thank-you for a couple of very important jobs.

Mom and Dad, as always, get the end credits. Thanks for the education, encouragement, and love. And for Kathy and the kids—Porter, Shelby, Courtney, and Aubrey—hugs and kisses.

Repro Rights

There is very little about this book that is truly formal, but at the insistence of our wise and esteemed counsel, let us declare: *No part of this book may be reproduced or utilized in any form or by any means, electronic or mechanical, including photocopying, recording, or by any information storage and retrieval system, without permission in writing from the publisher.* That would be us.

More Legal Stuff

Official disclaimer for you aspiring scientists and lab groupies. This is a hands-on science book. By the very intent of the design, you will be directed to use common, nontoxic, household items in a safe and responsible manner to avoid injury to yourself and others who are present while you are pursuing your quest for knowledge and enlightenment in the world of fluid dynamics. Just make sure that you have a fire blanket handy and a wall-mounted video camera to corroborate your story.

If, for some reason, perhaps even beyond your own control, you have an affinity for disaster, we wish you well. *But we, in no way take any responsibility for any injury that is incurred to any person using the information provided in this book or for any damage to personal property or effects that are directly or indirectly a result of the suggested activities contained herein.* Translation: You're on your own, despite the fact that many have preceded you in the the exploration of flight. Take heed from our friends who made the highlight reels while they pedaled off a cliff.

Less Formal Legal Stuff

If you happen to be a home schooler or very enthusiastic school teacher, please feel free to make copies of this book for your classroom or personal family use —one copy per student up to 35 students. If you would like to use an experiment from this book for a presentation to your faculty or school district, we would be happy to oblige. Just give us a whistle and we will send you a release for the particular lab activity you wish to use. Please contact us at the address below. Thanks.

Special Requests
Loose in the Lab, Inc.
9462 South 560 West
Sandy, Utah 84070

Table of Contents

National Content Standards (Grades K–4)
The position and motion of objects can be changed by pushing or pulling. The size of the change is related to the strength of the push or pull.

National Content Standards (Grades 5–8)
A. The motion of an object can be described by its position, direction of motion, and speed. That motion can be measured and represented on a graph.

B. An object that is not being subjected to a force will continue to move at a constant speed and in a straight line.

C. If more than one force acts on an object along a straight line, then the forces will reinforce or cancel one another, depending on their direction and magnitude. Unbalanced forces will cause changes in the speed or direction of an object's motion.

The Big Ideas & Lab Activities

Big Idea #1. Air is matter and matter takes up space.

Big Idea #2. When a force is applied to air, it can be compressed into a smaller space. When the force compressing the air is reduced or removed, the air tends to expand.

Big Idea #3. Cold air is more dense than hot air and will sink relative to hot air. Conversely, warm air is less dense than cold air and will rise relative to cold air.

Big Idea #4. Air pressure changes all the time and can be measured. Differences in air pressure can create forces in all directions.

Big Idea #5. We are completely surrounded by air and this air exerts pressure on all things. It can exert a force on matter and push it out of the way or sometimes change the shape or position of object.

Table of Contents

Big Idea #9. Newton's First Law. An object at rest, or in equilibrium, will remain in that state unless a force acts on that object to change its speed, shape, or direction of movement.

Big Idea #10. Force equals mass times acceleration. Or, the bigger it is and the faster it goes, the more it hurts when it hits.

Who Are You? And...

First of all, we may have an emergency at hand and we'll both want to cut to the chase and get the patient into the cardiac unit if necessary. So, before we go too much further, **define yourself.** Please check one and only one choice listed below and then immediately follow the directions that follow *in italics.* Thank you in advance for your cooperation.

I am holding this book because . . .

___ A. I am a responsible, but panicked, parent. My son/daughter/triplets (circle one) just informed me that his/her/their science fair project is due tomorrow. This is the only therapy I could afford on such short notice. Which means that if I was not holding this book, my hands would be encircling the soon-to-be-worm-bait's neck.

Directions: Can't say this is the first or the last time we heard that one. Hang in there, we can do this.

1. Quickly read the Table of Contents with the worm bait. The Big Ideas define what each section is about. Obviously, the kid is not passionate about science or you would not be in this situation. See if you can find an idea that causes some portion of an eyelid or facial muscle to twitch.

If that does not work, we recommend narrowing the list to the following labs because they are fast, use materials that can be acquired with limited notice, and the intrinsic level of interest is generally quite high.

How to Use This Book

2. Take the materials list from the lab write-up and page 199 of the Surviving a Science Fair Project section and go shopping.

3. Assemble the materials and perform the lab at least once. Gather as much data as you can.

4. Go to page 184 and start on Step 1 of Preparing Your Science Fair Project. With any luck you can dodge an academic disaster.

___ **B. I am worm bait.** My science fair project is due tomorrow and there is not anything moldy in the fridge. I need a big Band-Aid™, in a hurry.

Directions: Same as Option A. You can decide if and when you want to clue your folks in on your current dilemma.

___ **C. I am the parent of a student who informed me that he/ she has been assigned a science fair project due in six to eight weeks.** My son/daughter has expressed an interest in science books with humorous illustrations that attempt to explain air pressure and associated phenomena.

Who Are You ? And . . .

Directions: Well, you came to the right place.

A. *The first step is to have your kid or kids read through the Table of Contents and see if anything grabs their interest. Read through several experiments, see if the science teacher has any of the more difficult materials to acquire like glassware, the X-zylo, and sources of heat like a propane torch and ask if they can be borrowed. Ask them to play with the experiments and see which one really tickles their fancy.*

B. *After they have found and conducted the experiment that they like, have them take a peek at the Science Fair Ideas and see if they would like to investigate one of those or create an idea of their own. The guidelines for those are listed on page 188 in the Surviving Your Science Fair section. They have plenty of time so they can fiddle and fool with the original experiment and its derivations several times. Encourage them to work until they have an original question they want to answer and then start the process listed on page 190. They are well on their way to an excellent grade.*

___ D. I am a responsible student and have been assigned a science fair project due in six to eight weeks. I am interested in fluid dynamics and, despite demonstrating maturity and wisdom well beyond the scope of my peers, I too still have a sense of humor. Enlighten and entertain me.

Directions: Cool. Being teachers, we have heard reports of this kind of thing happening but usually in an obscure and hard to locate town several states removed. Nonetheless, congratulations.

Same as Option C. You have plenty of time and should be able to score very well. We'll keep our eyes peeled when the Nobel Prizes are announced in a couple of years.

How to Use This Book

___ E. I am a parent who home schools my child/children. We are always on the lookout for quality curriculum materials that are not only educationally sound but kid- and teacher-friendly. I am not particularly strong in science but I realize it is a very important topic. How is this book going to help me out?

Directions: In a lot of ways we created this book specifically for home schoolers.

1. We have taken the National Content Standards, the guidelines that are used by all public and private schools nationwide to establish their curriculum base, and listed them in the Table of Contents. You now know where you stand with respect to the national standards.

2. We then break these standards down and list the major ideas that you should want your kid to know. We call these the Big Ideas. Some people call them objectives, others call them curriculum standards, educational benchmarks, or assessment norms. Same apple, different name. The bottom line is that when your child is done studying this unit on light you want them to not only understand and explain each of the 10 ideas listed in this book, but also be able to defend and argue their position based on experiential evidence, hands-on science, that they have collected.

3. Building on the Big Ideas, we have collected and rewritten 50 hands-on science labs. Each one has been specifically selected so that it supports the Big Idea that it is correlated to. This is critical. If the kids do the science experiment, see it, smell it, touch it, and hear it, they will store that information in several places in their brains. When it comes time to comprehend the Big Idea, the concrete hands-on experiences provide the foundation for building the idea, which is quite often abstract. Kids who merely read about air pressure or pressure differentials, Bernoulli's law, and the effect of the shape of a wing on the lift that is generated are trying to build abstract ideas on abstract ideas and quite often miss the mark.

Who Are You? And...

For example: I can show you a recipe in a book for chocolate chip cookies and ask you to reiterate it. Or I can turn you loose in a kitchen, have you mix the ingredients, grease the pan, plop the dough on the cookie sheet, slide everything into the oven and wait impatiently until they pop out eight minutes later. Chances are that the description given by the person who actually made the cookies is going to be much better based on their true understanding of the process. **It is founded in experience.**

4. Once you have completed the experiment there are a number of extension ideas under the Science Fair Extensions that allow you to spend as much or as little time on the ideas as you deem necessary.

5. A word about humor. Science is not usually known for being funny even though Bill Nye The Science Guy, *Beaker from* Sesame Street, *and* Beakman's World *do their best to mingle the two. That's all fine and dandy but we want you to know that we incorporate humor because it is scientifically (and educationally) sound to do so. Plus it's really at the root of our personalities. Here's what we know:*

When we laugh . . .
a. Our pupils dilate, increasing the amount of light entering the eye.
b. Our heart rate increases, which pumps more blood to the brain.
c. Oxygen-rich blood to the brain means the brain is able to collect, process, and store more information. Big I.E. increased comprehension.
d. Laughter relaxes muscles, which can be involuntarily tense if a student is uncomfortable or fearful of an academic topic.
e. Laughter stimulates the immune system, which will ultimately translate into overall health and fewer kids will say they are sick of science.
f. Socially, it provides an acceptable pause in the academic routine, which then gives the student time to regroup and prepare to address some of the more difficult ideas with a renewed spirit. They can study longer and focus on ideas more efficiently.
g. Laughter releases chemicals in the brain that are associated with pleasure and joy.
6. If you follow the book in the order it is written you will be able to build ideas and concepts in a logical and sequential pattern. But that is by no means necessary. For a complete set of guidelines on our ideas on how to teach home-school kids science, check out our book, Why's the Cat on Fire? How to Excel at Teaching Science to Your Home Schooled Kids.

How to Use This Book

___ F. **I am a public/private school teacher** and this looks like an interesting book to add ideas to my classroom lesson plans.

Directions: It is, and please feel free to do so. However, while this is a great classroom resource for kids, may we also recommend two other titles Revenge of Kitty Hawk *if you wish to teach flight to 4th through 6th graders and* What's Up *for weather and related topics in the K–3 range.*

These two books have teacher preparation pages, student response sheets or lab pages, lesson plans, bulletin board ideas, discovery center ideas, vocabulary sheets, unit pretests, unit exams, lab practical exams, and student grading sheets. Basically everything you need if you are a science nincompoop, and a couple of cool ideas if you are seasoned veteran with an established curriculum. All of the ideas that are covered in this one book are covered much more thoroughly in the other two. They were specifically written for teachers.

___ G. **My son/daughter/grandson/niece/father-in-law** is interested in science and this looks like fun.

Directions: Congratulations on your selection. Add a gift certificate to the local science supply store and a package of hot chocolate mix and you have the perfect rainy Saturday afternoon gig.

___ H. **My flight club** has been talking about the effect of low pressure gradients traversing irregular geographic terrain patterns and the transitive forces exerted on the parallel universe. We were wondering if you could help us out.

Directions: Nope. Try the science fiction section of your library.

Lab Safety

Contained herein are 50 science activities to help you better understand the nature and characteristics of flight as we currently understand these things. However, since you are on your own in this journey we thought it prudent to share some basic wisdom and experience in the safety department.

Read the Instructions

An interesting concept, especially if you are a teenager. Take a minute before you jump in and get going to read all of the instructions as well as warnings. If you do not understand something, stop and ask an adult for help.

Clean Up All Messes

Keep your lab area clean. It will make it easier to put everything away at the end and may also prevent contamination and the subsequent germination of a species of mutant tomato bug larva. You will also find that chemicals perform with more predictability if they are not poisoned with foreign molecules.

Organize

Translation: Put it back where you get it. If you need any more clarification, there is an opening at the landfill for you.

Dispose of Poisons Properly

This will not be much of a problem with labs that use air as the primary lab material. However, if you happen to wander over into one of the many disciplines that incorporates the use of chemicals, then we would suggest that you use great caution with the materials and definitely dispose of any and all poisons properly.

Practice Good Fire Safety

If there is a fire in the room, notify an adult immediately. If an adult is not in the room and the fire is manageable, smother the outbreak with a fire blanket or use a fire extinguisher. When the fire is contained, immediately send someone to find an adult. If, for any reason, you happen to catch on fire, **REMEMBER: Stop, Drop, and Roll.** Never run; it adds oxygen to the fire, making it burn faster, and it also scares the bat guano out of the neighbors when they see the neighbor kid running down the block doing an imitation of a campfire marshmallow without the stick.

Protect Your Skin

It is a good idea to always wear protective gloves whenever you are working with chemicals. Again, this particular book does not suggest or incorporate chemicals in its lab activities very often. However, when we do, we are incorporating only safe, manageable kinds of chemicals for these labs. If you do happen to spill a chemical on your skin, notify an adult immediately and then flush the area with water for 15 minutes. It's unlikely, but if irritation develops, have your parents or another responsible adult look at it. If it appears to be of concern, contact a physician. Take any information that you have about the chemical with you.

Lab Safety

Save Your Nose Hairs

Sounds like a cause celebre LA style, but it is really good advice. To smell a chemical to identify it, hold the open container six to ten inches down and away from your nose. Make a clockwise circular motion with your hand over the opening of the container, "wafting" some of the fumes toward your nose. This will allow you to safely smell some of the fumes without exposing youself to a large dose of anything noxious. This technique may help prevent a nosebleed or your lungs from accidentally getting burned by chemicals.

Wear Goggles if Appropriate

If the lab asks you to heat or mix chemicals, be sure to wear protective eye wear. Also have an eyewash station or running water available. You never know when something is going to splatter, splash, or react unexpectedly. It is better to look like a nerd and be prepared than schedule a trip down to pick out a Seeing Eye™ dog. If you do happen to accidentally get chemicals in your eye, flush the area for 15 minutes. If any irritation or pain develops, immediately go see a doctor.

Lose the Comedy Routine

You should have plenty of time scheduled during your day to mess around but science lab is not one of them. Horseplay breaks glassware, spills chemicals, and creates unnecessary messes. Things that parents do not appreciate; trust us on this one.

No Eating

Do not eat while performing a lab. Putting your food in the lab area contaminates your food and the experiment. This makes for bad science and worse indigestion. Avoid poisoning yourself and goobering up your lab ware by observing this rule.

Happy and safe experimenting!

Recommended
Materials Suppliers

For every lesson in this book we offer a list of materials. Many of these are very easy to acquire and if you do not have them in your home already you will be able to find them at the local grocery or hardware store. For more difficult items we have selected, for your convenience, a small but respectable list of suppliers who will meet your needs in a timely and economical manner. Call for a catalog or quote on the item that you are looking for and they will be happy to give you a hand. Be sure to check out William Mark Corporation.

Loose in the Lab
9462 South 560 West
Sandy, Utah 84070
Phone 1-888-403-1189
Fax 1-801-568-9586
www.looseinthelab.com

Delta Education
80 NW Boulevard
Nashua, NH 03601
Phone 1-800-258-1302
Fax 1-800-282-9560
www.delta-ed.com

William Mark Corporation
112 N. Harvard Street
Claremont, Ca. 91711
Phone 1-800-620-0030
"Exceptional Flying Products"
www.x-zylo.com

Ward's Scientific
5100 W Henrietta Road
Rochester, New York 14692
Phone 800-387-7822
Fax 1-716-334-6174
www.wardsci.com

Educational Innovations
151 River Road
Cos Cob, Connecticut 06807
Phone 1-888-912-7474
Fax 1-203-629-2739
www.teachersource.com

Frey Scientific
100 Paragon Parkway
Mansfield, Ohio 44903
Phone 1-800-225-FREY
Fax 1-419-589-1546
www.freyscientific.com

Edmund Scientific
101 E. Gloucester Pike

Sargent Welch Scientific Co.
911 Commerce Court

The Ideas,
Lab Activities,
& Science Fair
Extensions

Big Idea 1

Air is matter and matter takes up space.

Submarine in a Cup

The Experiment

A dry napkin is inserted in an inverted dry, clear, glass full of air. This glass is then submerged, open side down, into a tank of water. The glass is left under water for 30 seconds. When it is removed from the water and the napkin is removed from the inside of the cup, it is still dry. What will they think of next?

Materials

1   Aquarium, sink, or large tub
1   Paper napkin
1   12-oz. clear, plastic drinking glass
    Water

Procedure

1. Fill the large container—either a sink, aquarium, or tub—full of water. Leave a little room near the top because you are going to not only dunk a cup but also your hand and a portion of your arm underwater. All of these things will displace an equivalent amount of water upward. Poor planning makes for a wet floor.

2. Ask a friend to assist you. Hand your friend the napkin and ask him or her to examine it. Your friend will most likely tell you that it is, among other things, dry. Stuff the dry napkin into the bottom of the clear, dry, plastic cup. Tip the cup upside down and make sure that the napkin does not fall out. You are ready to go.

3. Holding the cup upside down, place the rim evenly on the surface of the water in the large container. Gently push down on the cup until the entire cup is under water. Gently tilt the cup to the side, just a bit—not too much—notice what comes out of the cup. (Air would be the most appropriate answer, although, bubbles also works.)

4. Lift the cup back out of the container and ask your assistant to pull the napkin out of the cup. Have him or her examine it for wetness and announce his or her observation.

Data & Observations

Check one box: The napkin inside the cup was . . .

☐ Dry   ☐ Wet

How Come, Huh?

This lab introduces a basic idea about matter: Matter takes up space, and two things cannot occupy the same space at the same time. In this case, the two kinds of matter are air and water.

When the cup is flipped upside down, it traps air inside it. Air is matter, therefore air takes up space. As the cup, which is full of air, is placed on the surface of the water, it displaces the water directly under it. The reason this works is that the air is less dense than the water, so the air pushes down on the water and displaces it or moves it away from the inside of the cup.

In more basic terms, the cup is full of air. Air is matter and so is water, and they both take up space; but the air was there first, so there is no room inside the cup for the water.

Submarine in a Cup

Extension Ideas

1. Experiment with a variety of different fluids. Try cooking oil, rubbing alcohol, soda pop, and anything else that you can find around the house. Be sure to get the permission of your parents before you use anything other than water.

2. Determine if the temperature of the water has any effect at all on the outcome of this experiment.

3. Place a very small hole in the bottom of the plastic cup and repeat the experiment. After you make your observations, determine if there is a location on the cup where a hole would be permissible. In other words, where could you put a hole, submerse the cup, remove it 30 seconds later, and still have a dry napkin?

4. Do you have to use a napkin? Would a washcloth also work? How about a gerbil? Just kidding about the gerbil. Be nice to your pets and move on to the next lab before you get any bad ideas.

Pouring Air Underwater

The Experiment

We are going to build on the previous idea. A glass full of air is submerged into a tank of water, trapping the air inside. A second glass is submerged and filled with water. Without taking either glass out of water, you are going to be able to pour the air underwater from one glass to the other, filling it with air while underwater. And for an encore, pour it back again. This is a great follow-up to the last lab and another demonstration of the characteristics of matter.

Materials

1   Aquarium, sink, or large tub
2   12-oz. clear, drinking glasses
1   Straw
     Water

Procedure

1. Fill a large container—either sink, aquarium, or tub—full of water.

2. Dunk one cup into the water and let it fill up with water. Take another cup and push it into the water upside down so it traps a cup full of air underwater.

3. Holding the cup full of water upside down above the cup full of air, gently tip the cup full of air allowing bubbles to escape upward into the cup directly above it. Observe what happens.

Pouring Air Underwater

4. If you are pouring carefully, you will be able to continue to empty the cup of air into the cup of water. Air displaces the water in the top cup, and before you know it, you have a cup full of air—and you didn't even have to take it out of the water.

5. Reverse the process and see if you can pour the air back into the cup that it came from. Be careful not to spill any air, it is almost impossible to catch and get back into the cup.

6. Another way to fill the cup full of air is to hold a straw under the water and blow bubbles so that they rise up and are trapped inside the cup. Take a couple of deep breaths and you should be able to fill the entire cup.

How Come, Huh?

This lab reinforces the basic idea about matter introduced in the first lab: Matter takes up space, and two chunks of matter cannot occupy the same space at the same time.

The inverted drinking glass trapped the air inside when it was shoved under the water. However, air is less dense than water, and if it is free to move, it will be pushed to the surface by the buoyant force if given a chance to escape from the cup. So, when you tip the glass, the pressure is released, and the air molecules are pushed to the surface of the water, toward the second cup. As they enter the cup, they are trapped by the plastic again, so they start to displace or push water out of the cup so they have room to hang out. No two globs of matter, regardless of how small or large, can occupy the same physical space. This is beginning to sound familiar.

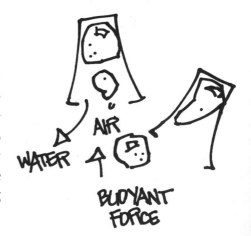

The same kind of thing happens with the straw. Your lungs push the air down the straw, but the second the air leaves the straw, it starts to expand and is pushed upward by the surrounding water, until it is trapped by the other cup where it displaces the water.

Extension Ideas

5. Again, as with the previous experiment, explore this same idea with a variety of different fluids. Try cooking oil, rubbing alcohol, soda pop, and anything else that you can find around the house. Be sure to get the permission of your parents before you use anything other than water.

6. Determine if the amount of water held by the cup has any effect at all on the outcome of this experiment. Or, is this principle independent of volume?

7. Place a very small hole in the bottom of the plastic cup and repeat the experiment. After you make your observations, determine if there is a location on the cup where a hole would be permissible. In other words, where could you put a hole and still be able to pour air from one container to another?

The Stubborn Balloon

The Experiment

This lab demonstrates that air takes up space, and if you want to replace that air with something else, you are going to have to figure out a way to let the air move out of the way.

This idea can be shown by inserting a rubber balloon into a clean, empty pop bottle. When you try to inflate the balloon, it simply will not cooperate no matter how hard you blow, until you make one small adaptation to your container.

Materials

1   Large tub
1   2-liter plastic bottle
1   Rubber balloon
1   Nail, 8 penny
1   Lungs, healthy
    Air

Procedure

1. Wiggle the balloon down inside the bottle and stretch the opening of the balloon over the mouth of the bottle forming a complete seal. The balloon should be completely inside the bottle with the exception of the rubber stretched over the neck.

2. Take a deep breath, place the bottle in your mouth and blow into it as hard as you can. Your objective is to try to inflate the balloon while it is still inside the bottle. Stop just short of passing out or turning scarlet.

BALLOON

2-LITER BOTTLE

3. We are guessing that you did not have much success. Take the nail and use it to create a small hole near the bottom of the bottle. Remove the nail.

4. Take another deep breath, hold the bottle to your mouth again and blow into it once more. You should notice a slightly different reaction for your efforts this time.

5. To help you understand what is going on repeat the experiment and hold your finger near the hole at the bottom of the bottle while you inflate the balloon. You should notice a small, but noticeable stream of air coming out of the bottle.

Data & Observations

Record your observations in the spaces provided below by circling the reaction that you observed in each circumstance.

Experiment #	Inflated?	
1 • No Hole	Yes	No
2 • Hole	Yes	No

The Stubborn Balloon

How Come, Huh?

When you covered the opening of the bottle with the balloon, you were trapping the air inside the bottle. Air is matter, and it takes up space. When you blew into the bottle, you were trying to force more air into an already full bottle. Since there was no more room, the air inside the bottle pushed back on the balloon when you were trying to inflate it and said, "Sorry, try someplace else, we're full." Same kind of problem that Mary and Joseph encountered just not as well recorded for some reason. At any rate, the balloon did not inflate despite your best efforts.

By putting a hole in the bottom of the bottle you were creating an escape route for the air molecules inside the bottle. The second time you blew into the bottle the air inside the balloon pushed on the air inside the bottle, and those air molecules said, "OK, if you insist on being in here we'll leave and go play in the room." They exited the bottle through the small hole and made room for the balloon to expand.

Extensions

8. If you want to have some fun with your friends, take this bottle with the hole and bet them that you can inflate the balloon in the bottle and that they can't. The one rule is that you hold the bottle at all times. To start the bet you blow into the bottle and leave your finger off the hole. The balloon will inflate. Then when it is time for your friend to try, discreetly put your finger back over the hole, blocking the air inside the bottle. They will blow and blow and nothing will happen. You can take the bottle back, remove your finger, inflate the bottle, and look at them with chagrined disbelief that they couldn't blow a little, tiny balloon up.

The Persnickety Stopper

The Experiment

This lab builds on the previous three labs and, again, demonstrates that air takes up space; and if you want to replace that air, you are going to have to figure out a device to let it move out of the way. This device is usually called a valve.

In this lab we have two stoppers. The first one has two holes and the second one has just a single hole. A funnel is inserted into each stopper, and water is added. The first stopper lets the water rush in without a problem. The second stopper, with only one hole, is very persnickety and will only allow a couple of drops of water. You should already have this one figured out.

Materials

2   2-liter bottles
1   12-oz. drinking glass
1   #3, one-hole, rubber stopper
1   #3, two-hole, rubber stopper
2   Funnels, liquid, narrow tip
    Water

Procedure

1. Insert one stopper in each bottle and place one funnel in a hole in the stopper in each bottle.

The Persnickety Stopper

2. Begin with the bottle that has the stopper with two holes. Pour a little bit of water into the funnel and observe what happens.

3. Now pour water into the funnel that has only one hole and compare the results that you observed in the first experiment.

4. Finally, grab the bottle with the two-hole stopper. Place your finger over the hole that does not have the funnel in it and fill the funnel with water. Observe the difference in reaction this time, create a cognitive note, and head for the How Come, Huh? section to see if your explanation matches ours.

How Come, Huh?

When you stoppered the bottles, you were creating a very narrow pathway for air and water to move in and out of the bottles. In the first experiment you were using a *two*-hole stopper, so there were two pathways for air and water to move in and out of the bottle. When you poured the water into the funnel, gravity started to pull down on it and it entered the bottle. Because it is heavier than air, it pushed, or displaced the air upward through the second hole in the stopper, which was acting as a very simple valve. So, as the water went down one hole, an equivalent volume of air was pushed up the other. The same thing happens when you sit in a tub full of water. As you sit down, the water around rises and moves out of your way.

When you inserted the funnel in the *one*-hole stopper, you had a different situation completely. The water in the funnel was being pulled down by gravity, but when it got to the stopper, it was running into a bottle full of air. Air is matter and matter takes up space. Even though the water is more dense than the air, the air—when it was being squished by the water—compressed just enough to be able to push back on the water and say, "Sorry, there's no room in here for you, we're full." This explanation is predicated on the fact that you actually believe that air and water molecules can talk to one another.

Finally, when you placed your finger over the second hole in the two-hole stopper, you were essentially creating another one-hole stopper. The air could not escape, the water was not heavy enough to push the air out of the water, so this bottle became persnickety all of a sudden too. The same kind of thing happens when you go to put water into the small hole of a squirt gun. You hold the gun under the stream of water in your kitchen sink, and if the water is trying to rush in too fast, the air inside the gun will push back on it, and it will be harder to fill your gun.

Extensions

9. Take a clean, dry, 2-liter pop bottle and write— using a thick, black marker—DO NOT OPEN, on the side of the bottle.

Place the bottle in a sink and fill it with water. When it is completely full, cap the bottle, dry it off, and set it out on the counter where people will notice it.

Eventually someone will take note of the bottle and uncap it, out of curiosity. Figure out what happens next and also be able to explain why it did.

Big Idea 2

When a force is applied to air; it can be compressed into a smaller space. When the force compressing the air is reduced or removed, the air tends to expand.

The Petulant Eyedropper

The Experiment

You are going to construct a toy that allows you to directly observe the compression and expansion of air inside a glass eyedropper in response to external pressure.

Not only does this lab explain Big Idea #2, but it also give you a clearer understanding of how submarines work and even why hot air balloons prefer to take their customers for rides on cold, autumn mornings. Ah, the mysteries of nature, splashed with commercial implications all wrapped up in technology. It's a wonderful world.

Materials

1   2-liter bottle, empty, with lid
1   Glass eyedropper
1   12-oz. glass
    Water

Procedure

1. Fill the 2-liter pop bottle full of water, right up to the top.

2. Squeeze the rubber bulb off the top of the eyedropper and dunk the glass end piece into the cup of water. Replace the bulb over the glass piece while the entire eyedropper is still underwater.

The Petulant Eyedropper

3. Let the eyedropper full of water float in the cup of water. If it sinks to the bottom of the glass, it is too heavy to use. Gently squeeze the bulb and drive a little water out of the glass portion and place it in the water again.

You only have to squeeze a little bit of water out. If you squeeze too much, then you will find that the eyedropper is very buoyant and much harder to get to sink to the bottom of the bottle. Experimentation is the best way to figure out what exactly is going on.

4. When you get an eyedropper that floats at the top of the glass, you are ready to place it in the pop bottle and screw the cap on firmly. When you are all set to experiment, it will look like the illustration at the right.

5. Now it is time to experiment. Watch the water level inside the eyedropper carefully as you squeeze the sides of the bottle with both hands. The more pressure you put on the sides of the bottle, the more water goes inside the eyedropper. When the eyedropper becomes less buoyant than the surrounding water, it will start to sink to the bottom of the bottle. When your eyedropper gets to the bottom of the bottle, gently release some of the pressure and observe what happens to the water level.

6. With some experimentation, you can get the eyedropper to behave exactly the way that you want it to. Squeeze it hard enough to get it to fall and then stop it midway down. Let it rise and then freeze it in position. Squeeze the bottle again and just before it hits the bottom of the pop bottle get it to stop.

How Come, Huh?

When you placed your hands on the bottle and squeezed, the pressure inside the bottle increased. This extra pressure immediately started to squeeze the water molecules inside the bottle—they were not exactly tickled pink about this new pressure so they looked for a place to go. Liquids do not compress or squish as easily as gases, so the water molecules squeezed the air molecules into the eyedropper.

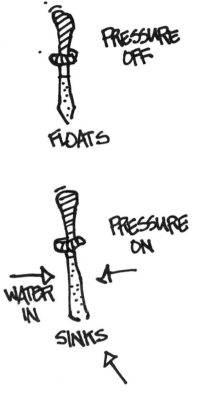

When this happened, water was forced into the eyedropper. The eyedropper was now heavier. This added weight made the eyedropper more dense than the surrounding water, which, in turn, caused it to sink. When the pressure was released, the gases expanded to a more comfortable spacing, the water was pushed back out and the eyedropper became less dense and more buoyant—enough to rise to the surface again.

Extensions

10. Tell your friends that you have a new breathalizer that can instantly tell when a person has stinky breath. Have your friend blow on the bottle while you hold it. Squeeze the bottle and the eyedropper sinks to the bottom of the bottle. Tell them that to cut back on the garlic mints.

11. You can pretend to magnetize the finger of your friend with a bar magnet, similar to the way that you would magnetize a nail. Have them place their "magnetized" finger on the bottle and move it slowly toward the bottom of the bottle. Follow their finger with the eyedropper and have them figure out how you did it.

Expectorating Bottle

The Experiment

A bottle full of water and air is stoppered with a straw sticking out of the top. You know that air can be compressed from the previous experiment and also that air expands when the pressure squishing it into a smaller place is released. Both of these ideas are illustrated again in a very vivid and memorable way.

The result is both humorous and educational, especially if you are the one who is watching.

Materials

1   Empty, 2-liter pop bottle
1   #3, one-hole stopper
1   Plastic straw
1   Jar of petroleum jelly
    Water
1   Pair of goggles
2   Lungs
1   Pretty good sense of humor

Procedure

1. Find a clean, empty, 2-liter bottle and fill it with water; leave 2 inches of air at the top. This 2 inches is critical because you need to be able to compress the air inside the bottle.

2. Holding the stopper in one hand, slide the straw about one-third of the way into it. If you are having a bit of trouble getting the straw to slide into the stopper, use a dab of petroleum jelly.

3. Insert the stopper and straw apparatus into the neck of the bottle, leaving the tallest part of the straw sticking up. Use the illustration to the left as a guide.

4. Take a deep breath and blow into the straw until you can no longer force any more air into the bottle. When the bottle starts to win, quickly remove your face.

5. Look down the center of the straw into the bottle.

How Come, Huh?

When you blow into the straw, you are cramming billions of extra air molecules into the bottle, which significantly increases the air and water pressure inside the bottle. At the same time the balance of forces has just been altered.

Getting crammed into a smaller space must irritate the air particles. They don't have as much room as they used to, so they push on each other and at the same time they also push down on the water molecules. This causes an increase in the pressure inside the bottle, both in the air and in the air pushing down on the surface of the water.

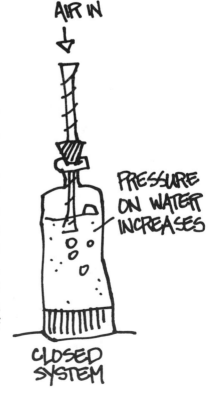

AIR IN

PRESSURE ON WATER INCREASES

CLOSED SYSTEM

Expectorating Bottle

It is the pushing of the air molecules down on the surface of the water that forces some of the water up into the straw and out into the air where they proceed to dampen your once dry table. This fountain of water continues until there is once again a balance of air pressure inside and out of the bottle and everybody has their space. You can always tell when this happens because the water stops being pushed out of the bottle.

Extensions

12. Experiment with the diameter of the straw and compare that with the height of the water shooting out of the bottle. Keep all of the other variables constant.

13. Determine the optimum ratio of air to water in the bottle to produce the highest stream of water shooting out of the bottle.

14. Experiment and see if the size of the bottle has any effect on the distance that the water shoots up and out of the straw.

15. If you live in a mountainous area where it is easy to change elevation, design an experiment that explores the effect of air pressure and elevation on the height that the water shoots out of the bottle.

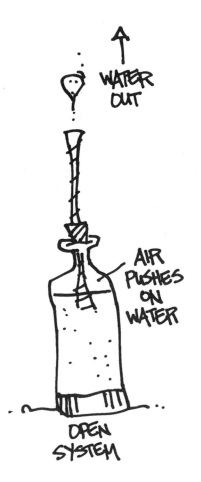

Medical Marshmallows

THIS WON'T HURT A BIT.

The Experiment

This experiment is the reverse of the previous two. Instead of increasing the pressure on the air molecules and squishing them into a smaller space, you are going to reduce the air pressure on the air molecules and allow them to expand. Opposites day at the lab.

Materials

1   Marshmallow, small
1   Syringe, large
1   Metric ruler
1   Planet with atmospheric pressure

Procedure

1. Place the marshmallow in the box on page 42. Trace around the perimeter of the marshmallow and measure the maximum distance across.

2. Remove the stem from the syringe and place the marshmallow inside the cylinder. Replace the stem and holding the tip toward the ceiling, slide the stem inside the syringe until it touches the marshmallow.

3. Place your thumb or some clay over the opening of the syringe, blocking any air that might enter through that opening, and quickly pull the plunger (stem) of the syringe out.

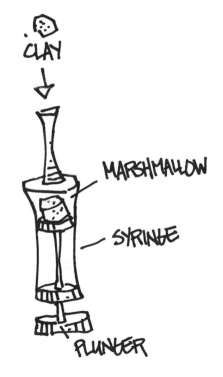

CLAY

MARSHMALLOW

SYRINGE

PLUNGER

Medical Marshmallows

4. Observe what happens to the marshmallow when the amount of air inside the syringe stays the same, but the volume increases dramatically. Place the marshmallow inside the syringe over the second box in the Observations section, and trace and measure the maximum diameter of the expanded marshmallow.

5. Move the plunger in and out several times and observe what happens to the marshmallow as the volume of air inside the container increases and decreases.

Data & Observations

Trace, measure, and record the diameter of each marshmallow in the space provided below. Measure the diameter using metric units not inches.

Beginning Marshmallow   Expanded Marshmallow

How Come, Huh?

By placing the marshmallow inside the syringe and then re-placing the plunger and plugging up the other end with the clay or your thumb, you were creating a closed system. Nothing could get out and nothing could get in.

The marshmallow was in a state of equilibrium, or balance, when you first created this situation. However, when you pulled the plunger out, you were giving the air molecules inside the plunger more space and at the same time reducing the average density of the air molecules. In other words, they had more room to spread out.

As the air molecules inside the syringe spread out, the amount of pressure on the marshmallow decreased. Marshmallows are made by trapping air inside sugar. If the air surrounding the marshmallow is not pushing as hard on the marshmallow, the air trapped inside the marshmallow can expand also—which is what you saw. When you squished the plunger back down, the air pressure increased again. The air inside the marshmallow got squished and it returned to its original size.

Extensions

16. Borrow a vacuum pump from your local science class and try this same experiment using the pump. You can also use things like partially inflated balloons, styrofoam peanuts, and other items that have air inside them.

17. Try the same experiment with packing peanuts or soft pieces of styrofoam. They are made the same way that marshmallows are, by injecting air into a material, so logic would dictate that you would get the same results. Or will you?

Big Idea 3

Cold air is more dense than hot air and will sink relative to hot air. Conversely, warm air is less dense than cold air and will rise relative to cold air.

Bubble Slide

The Experiment

Cold air is more dense than warm air. We are going to demonstrate this using a gas that is colder and denser than air—carbon dioxide.

Here we go, soap bubbles are blown into the air over a cardboard box. They are pulled down into the box full of dry ice. The funny thing is that they do not sink to the bottom of the aquarium, but instead, they mysteriously float and bounce in the middle of the box, supported by a gas that is much denser than air.

Now comes the fun part. The bubbles are floating on the gas. You whip down the secret trapdoor that you have built and the bubbles slide right out of the box and on to the floor.

Materials

1   Cardboard box, sink size or so
1   Pound of dry ice
1   Hammer
1   Bottle of bubble solution with wand
1   Pair of gloves
1   Cloth or paper bag
1   Kitchen knife
1   Roll of masking tape
1   Pair of goggles (optional)
1   Bucket
    Adult Supervision

Bubble Slide

Procedure

1. To prepare your box, take the kitchen knife and cut down both sides of one end. Bend the end flap up and down a couple of times to make sure that it is relatively flexible. Tape the end flap up so that the box appears whole, and in one piece. As an alternative you can use a 10-gallon aquarium. An aquarium allows you to see the bubbles better but is harder to handle when pouring them out on to the ground.

2. *With adult supervision,* put your gloves on and set the dry ice on a hard surface. Cover it with a cloth or insert it in a paper bag, and smash it into little pieces with the hammer. Again, with gloved hands, either empty the piece of dry ice directly from the bag into the box or remove the cover, pick up the dry ice pieces and place them in the box. *Dry ice is 109 degrees Fahrenheit below zero. If you touch it with bare hands, you run the risk of freezing the skin cells solid, which tends to kill them instantly. Be safe and use the gloves. You will avoid a lot of pain and the unsightly appearance of greenish-black fingers.*

3. Allow the dry ice pieces to stand undisturbed in the bottom of the box for a couple of minutes. Dry ice is the solid form of carbon dioxide. At room temperature, dry ice undergoes a process called *sublimation*, changing directly from a solid to a gas. As you wait, the box will fill up with this invisible carbon dioxide gas. Because carbon dioxide is heavier than air, it displaces, or pushes the air up and out of the box.

4. After two or three minutes, take the bubble solution and blow bubbles *over* the top of the box so that they float down into it. Do not blow down into the box or you will blow the gas out of the container. Observe the bubbles. This is where they get weird. The carbon dioxide in the tank is heavier than the air trapped in the bubbles, so they look like spheres bobbing up and down on an invisible ocean of gas—which, curiously enough, is exactly what is happening.

5. Fill the box with bubbles, and then gently remove the end flap. The bubbles will "ride" the heavier carbon dioxide gas out of the box and onto the floor.

OXYGEN
MOLECULE
(O_2)

6. Allow the gas to accumulate in the aquarium again and then blow more bubbles. When you have 10 to 15 bubbles floating on the layer of carbon dioxide, gently tip the box back and forth. As the carbon dioxide sloshes back and forth, the motion of the gas will be recorded in the movement of the bubbles on the surface of the gas.

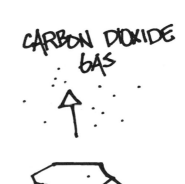

CARBON DIOXIDE
GAS

7. Take a bucket, place a couple of pieces of dry ice in the bucket, using gloved hands, and then pour the gas from the bucket into the aquarium when there are bubbles floating on the surface. As the level of carbon dioxide increases, the height of the bubbles inside the container will get higher and higher.

SOLID
CARBON DIOXIDE

Bubble Slide

How Come, Huh?

Dry ice is solid carbon dioxide—a substance that is usually a gas at room temperature. When the dry ice is placed in the tank, it sublimes, which means that it changes directly from a solid to a gas without ever becoming a liquid. As the dry ice changes to a gas (one that is heavier than air, we might add), it starts to fill the tank. Remember that two chunks of matter can't occupy the same space? Same deal here. The carbon dioxide is heavier— check out the illustrations to the right— so it pushes the lighter air out of the tank.

OXYGEN MOLECULE (O_2)

When the bubbles—full of air—fall into the box, they stop when they hit the layer of heavier carbon dioxide—just like tossing a piece of wood on the water. It just floats. The bubbles look like they are floating because the gas inside the tank behaves like a liquid and is moving constantly.

CARBON DIOXIDE MOLECULE (CO_2)

When you dropped the flap on the box, the heavier, colder air rushed out of the box. You couldn't see the air, but you could see the bubbles riding the carbon dioxide. Air masses move in much the same way, and this is what is responsible for creating wind.

Science Fair Extensions

18. You can demonstrate the density of the gas, carbon dioxide, and the role of oxygen in combustion at the same time. With adult supervision, light a votive candle and place it on the edge of a rain gutter. Using gloved hands, take an empty bucket and fill it full of carbon dioxide by scooping it into the box you have prepared (or an aquarium). Gently pour the carbon dioxide directly from the cup into the rain gutter, so it runs down into the flame of the candle and extinguishes it immediately.

Colliding "Air" Masses

The Experiment

In this experiment an aquarium is divided down the middle with a sheet of cardboard. One side of the aquarium is filled with cold water that will be dyed blue, and the other side is filled with hot water that will have red dye added to it.

When the cardboard is removed, the water from the two halves of the aquarium will mix and produce an interesting effect that can be used to explain the occurrence of winds, ability of hot air balloons to function, and a host of other phenomena.

Materials

1   10-gallon aquarium
1   Sheet of cardboard, large enough to separate the aquarium
1   Red/blue pencil
1   Bottle of red food coloring
1   Lead pencil
1   Bottle of blue food coloring
1   Ruler
    Cold water, 5 gallons
    Hot water, 5 gallons

Colliding "Air" Masses

Procedure

1. Place the cardboard in the center of the aquarium. It does not have to be watertight, but it should fit snugly against the sides and rise all the way to the top, separating the tank into two halves.

2. Fill one side with very cold water and then add several drops of blue food coloring, mixing the whole concoction with the ruler. This is your cold air mass.

3. Now fill the other side with very hot water and add several drops of red food coloring, which is also mixed in with the ruler. Voila, hot air mass.

4. Draw an illustration of what the tank looks like with the two liquids separated. Use your red/blue pencil to make the illustration. Record the time as 0 minutes.

Time: _____

5. When you are ready, quickly remove the sheet of cardboard. Your job is to watch what happens to the two "air masses" as they collide. Record you observations in the space on the next page at one minute, three minutes, and five minutes.

6. When you are done, empty the aquarium contents down the sink and wipe up any messes

Data & Observations

Draw a picture of what happens to the two air masses in the spaces provided on pages 52 and 53. Record your observations at one, three, and five minutes.

How Come, Huh?

The cold water is more dense than the warm water. When the cardboard was removed, the heavier water sank and pushed the warmer, less dense water upward. The interface turned purple and represents a layer of clouds.

One Minute

Three Minutes

Five Minutes

Seven Minutes

Ten Minutes

Fifteen Minutes

Convection Currents

The Experiment

There are several ways to approach this idea of hot air and cold air and which sinks while the other rises.

In this particular experiment we are going to recommend a commercially produced glass tube that we have available in our catalog and on our web site. The tube looks like a giant, fat "O" and has an opening at the top where you add water and a drop of food coloring.

Once the tube is filled you light a votive candle—adult supervision, as always, recommended— and you heat one side of the "O". As the water is heated, it starts to flow in a convection current.

Materials

1   Convection tube
1   Votive candle
1   Bottle of food coloring
    Water
    Adult Supervision

Procedure

1. Fill the convection tube with room-temperature water. Add two or three drops of food coloring to one side of the convection tube and try not to disturb the food coloring.

2. With the supervision of an adult, light a votive candle and hold the side of the tube that has the food coloring directly over the candle flame. Use the illustration below as a guide.

3. Observe what happens as the water on that side of the tube is heated.

How Come, Huh?

As the water was heated, it absorbed the energy from the burning candle. This caused the molecules of water to move back and forth and bounce around more than the molecules of water that were not being heated by the candle. All this bouncing around caused the same number of molecules to take up more space. This makes the water less dense. The less dense water was lighter than the cold water and started to rise. As the warm water rose, it left a void and that void was filled by cold water. The cold water got warmer, the warm water got cooler, and this created a convection current.

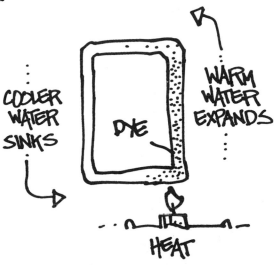

Extensions

19. Find other containers that can be heated on one side and set up a convection current.

20. Convection currents can also be established using hot and cold air. Create a replica of this experiment using air instead of water with smoke as the indicator, instead of food coloring. Be sure to get adult supervision.

Convection Tube

The Experiment

You are going to heat a folded piece of metal-alloy screen stuffed into one end of a large diameter steel tube with a propane torch. When the torch is removed, the tube begins to hum. If you tilt the tube sideways—giving the illusion that you are "pouring" the sound out of the tube—the sound will stop. If you quickly hold the tube in a vertical position, the sound will resume.

Materials

1   Propane torch or Bunsen burner
1   Propane torch stand
1   Ignitor or book of matches
1   Oven mitt
1   Steel tube, 19" x 1.5", with metal-alloy screen, 2" x 6"
1   Hammer
1   Large, opaque, plastic cup
1   Pair of goggles
1   Wooden dowel or screwdriver
    Adult supervision

Procedure

1. These tubes are easy and relatively inexpensive to make. Head to the plumbing or hardware section of your local handyman's store, and tell them you are a science enthusiast and explain the experiment. (If you get the right guy, he will either reduce the price or give you pieces of scrap pipe to play with for free.) The pipe is a section of the fence post that holds up a metal fence. The screen is a 20 gauge metal alloy that can be cut into a 2" by 6" strip, trifolded into a 2" by 2" square, and then pounded into the bottom of the pipe using a wooden dowel and hammer.

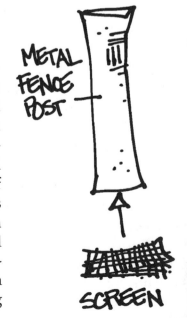

METAL FENCE POST

SCREEN

2. With your goggles on and an adult by your side, fire up the torch and put the oven mitt on the hand that is going to hold the tube. Hate to state the apparent and obvious, but you would be surprised at some of the questions we get.

3. The key to this experiment is to get the screen inside the bottom of the tube red hot using the torch. To achieve that end, you are going to want to hold the tube upright with the metal-alloy screen toward the end nearest the torch. Use the illustration above as a guide.

4. Insert the flame of the torch into the bottom of the tube so that it is heating the alloy screen directly. When the screen gets hot enough, the tube will begin to hum, _but not until you remove the flame from inside the tube_. This usually takes about 15 to 20 seconds. Every tube is different, so it would be a good idea to practice and time your particular tube before you uncork this one on your friends.

At any rate, when the screen is hot enough, the tube starts to hum, eyeballs bug out, and your friends are really impressed. Don't stop now; it's zinger time. Pick up the large, opaque, plastic cup. Hold the cup up and tilt the tube at an angle, so that it looks like you are literally "pouring" the sound from the tube into the cup. The interesting thing is that as soon as you tip the tube over the sound ceases.

Convection Tube

5. Quickly return the tube to its upright position and "pour" the sound back into the tube from the cup, and it will start to hum again. As with comedy, omelettes, and good science demos, timing is everything, so practice before you do this at the family reunion.

Data & Observations

Try rotating the pipe to different positions while it is humming. Circle the positions that produce sound and put an X through those that do not.

How Come, Huh?

Touch a lit propane torch to anything, and it's a sure bet that it is going to get hot. As the hot screen heats the air inside the tube, a convection current starts to form and the air rises through the tube. The air escaping from the top of the tube creates an area of low pressure just above the screen, and cold air enters the bottom of the tube. As it passes through the hot screen, it is heated rapidly and starts to rise turbulently through the tube. This turbulent motion produces a wave of vibrating air molecules that our ears interpret as a hum.

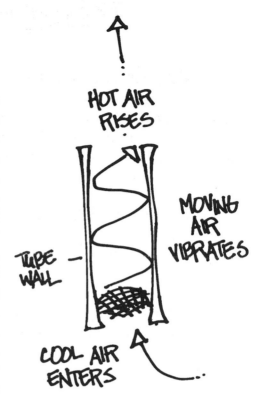

When you tip the tube sideways, you disrupt the movement of the air. Because air molecules don't get a chance to bounce around inside the tube and produce the vibrations, the sound ceases. By returning the tube to its vertical position, the air is free to rise and produce sound again. For the record, you cannot pour sound. It's an illusion— that is, if it is well done. That's where the practice comes in.

Extensions

21. Make a set of pipes using different lengths and diameters of pipe. Again, the hardware store will have a variety of different pipes, made out of different materials. Determine how these two variables affect the pitch that is produced.

22. Find out if the local church has a set of organ pipes— same concept, slightly more refined. Create an experiment that allows you to replicate a church organ pipe.

Ring of Fire

The Experiment

In the previous experiment we heard the effect of heating a screen, which produced a convection current in a long metal tube. In this lab we are actually going to be able to see how the convection current moves by watching the behavior of an empty tea bag— that has been lit on fire and is burning.

The bag produces a column of hot air, and when the weight of the bag allows it to be lifted up with the rising current of hot air, you have a floating flammable tea bag. This is one of those labs that you do with an adult around—mostly, because grown-ups get a kick out of this stuff too.

Materials

1 Tea bag, paper
1 Pie tin
1 Book of matches
   Goggles (optional)
   Adult Supervision

Procedure

DO THIS ACTIVITY OUTSIDE WHERE THERE IS NO DANGER OF ANYTHING CATCHING ON FIRE. You will also want to have an **adult** around to help out.

1. Open the top of the tea bag and discard the contents of the bag.

2. Open the tea bag up so that it forms a cylinder and place it in the center of the pie tin.

3. Under the supervision of an adult, light a match and touch it to the top of the tea bag in several places so that it begins to burn from the top down. Stand back and observe what happens.

How Come, Huh?

As the tea bag burned, the air directly above the bag was heated. Hot air rises, so it headed up and out leaving a vacancy. Cooler air replaced the hot air that rose toward the ceiling, and it too was heated by the burning tea bag. Off to the ceiling and a convection current was created.

At a certain time in the experiment the mass of the tea bag had burned down to the point where it could be carried aloft by this current of hot air and so it lifted off the tin. Because it continued to burn as it floated, it perpetuated the convection current until all of the paper had been consumed. The ash then cooled and fell to the ground.

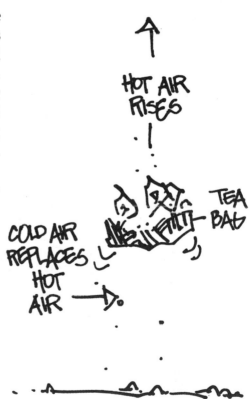

Extensions

23. Under adult supervision, experiment with other very light papers, like wrapping tissue, mimeograph separation sheets, and single-ply toilet paper.

Solar Balloon

The Experiment

There are several solar hot air balloons available commercially. We enjoy using a balloon manufactured by Delta Education. You can catch up with them at www.delta-edu.com or call toll free at 1-800-258-1302.

The balloon inflates to about 12 feet. This is the part where you use your lungs. The balloon is then tied off and placed in the direct sunlight. The black, solar balloon collects and absorbs the sunlight, further heating the air inside, causing it to expand. When the balloon reaches a density that is lighter than the surrounding air, it starts to float.

Materials

1   Solar, hot air balloon
1   Sunny day
1   20-foot string
    Air

Procedure

1. Stretch the balloon out in front of you and start to inflate the balloon by blowing into it.

2. When the balloon is completely inflated, tie it off and take it to a nice, sunny location. The black plastic will immediately begin to absorb the heat energy from the sun, and the air inside the balloon will start to expand.

3. You will notice the balloon starting to float. When the air inside the balloon becomes less dense than the air outside the balloon, it will float into the air and be tethered only by the string.

How Come, Huh?

When the difference in density between the air inside the solar balloon and the air outside the balloon gets large enough, the balloon starts to float. The reason for this is that the air molecules expand when they are heated. The expanded air is pushed up by the heavier, denser air outside the balloon.

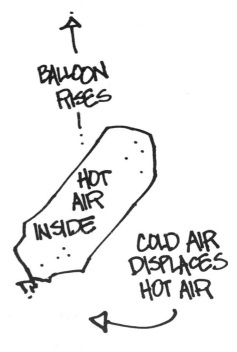

Extensions

24. There are several patterns for tissue paper hot air balloons. These balloons are usually inflated using a hair dryer and kept aloft by burning a small amount of alcohol and constantly filling the balloon with hot air. Be sure to get the permission of an adult to do this.

25. Substitute a dark plastic garbage bag for the solar hot air balloon and see if you can figure a way to get that in the air.

Big Idea 4

Air pressure changes all the time and can be measured. Differences in air pressure can create forces in all directions.

Oatmeal Blaster

The Experiment

Air. . . we can't live without it, and we can't see it, but we can "see" it is there by sending things through it. Confused yet? There's more. We need air, and if we don't respire, we expire. Definitely a case for cause and effect if there ever was one. By creating and using an air cannon, you can experiment with the movement of air. These are called compression waves.

In this lab we are going to convert an ordinary, old, empty, unloved, used oatmeal container into a semi-high-tech pneumatic blaster than can knock down paper dummies and extinguish candle flames from a distance of up to five feet. Cool.

Materials

1   Oatmeal container, empty
1   Pair of scissors
1   Pencil
1   U.S. dime
1   Metric ruler
        and
1   Book of matches
1   Candle, votive
        or
1   Paper target
     Adult supervision

Procedure

1. Remove the lid from your container and make sure that all of the contents have been removed. (Dump any leftover oatmeal into the garbage can.)

Oatmeal Blaster

2. Place the container upside down on the table. Put the dime in the center of the container and trace around it using the pencil. Set the dime aside.

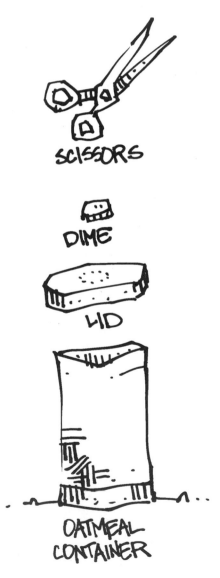

SCISSORS

DIME

LID

OATMEAL CONTAINER

3. Using the point of one of the scissor blades gently insert the scissors into the cardboard and make a small hole in the center of the circle that you drew around the dime. Once the blade is inside the container, snip a small hole, following the outline of the dime as a guide.

4. Replace the cardboard lid on the top of the container. The lid is now known as the "thumping zone." When you are asked to hit it, whap it directly in the center by flicking your middle finger with your thumb. If it helps, make an X in the center of the lid. Your super snuffer is now ready.

5. Place your super snuffer on the table and mark the opening with a small piece of masking tape. From the edge of the tape, measure 15 centimeters and place the candle or the target found on page 69. Aim the opening at the target. Holding the top of the container with one hand, give the thumping zone a whap by flicking it with your center finger just like you would flick a booger off your finger.

Procedure

6. If the flame was extinguished or your target tipped over, place an *x* in the 15-centimeter column. "Shoot" at the target three times from each distance. Record your observations each time and if you hit it two out of three times, then mark the box under the distance. Move the target back 5 centimeters and shoot again. If you are having trouble visualizing this, there is an illustration right above that should help. Repeat this until you can no longer extinguish the flame or tip the target over.

Data & Observations

Experiment with knocking over the target, found on page 69, or extinguishing the candle flame and recording the distances that you were able to achieve in the data table below by marking an *x*.

Distance (cm)						
Trial 1						
Trial 2						
Trial 3						

Oatmeal Blaster

How Come, Huh?

As the "thumping zone" is struck, the air molecules inside the container are compressed or pushed together. Just like squeezing a balloon full of air, the air is searching for a place to go. In this case the air found a hole. The hole gave the air under pressure a place and direction to go. The air comes rushing out with great energy, focused in a narrow wave traveling at high speed. When this wave of air encounters the target, it blows it over; when it comes in contact with the candle flame, the flame is extinguished.

Extensions

26. Vary the hole size in the air cannon to see if it has any effect on the kind of air wave it sends out.

27. Vary the material used to strike to send the air wave. The rubbery kinds of material work well, but try others. . . plastic, cardboard. Vary the thickness of material. Let your imagination run wild.

28. Finally, size does matter. Make a super snuffer using a 5-gallon bucket, small garbage can, or other container. Cut a hole in one end and set your target up at the other end of the garage. Have fun and experiment with different materials for the thumping zone as well as optimizing the size of the hole in the front of the snuffer.

Blaster Target

Pushy Index Cards

The Experiment

A glass half full of water is covered with an ordinary index card. No adhesives of any kind are used to fix the card to the glass, it is simply sitting right on top of the rim of the glass.

The card and the glass are inverted, and the water remains inside the glass—another victory for air pressure. Now repeat the experiment, holding the card over the head of a volunteer.

Materials

1   8-12 ounce drinking glass
1   Index card, 4" by 6"
1   Unsuspecting assistant
    Water

Procedure

1.   Fill the glass three-fourths full of water. If you want to add an element of drama to this, ask your friends to examine the surface of the cup for adhesives, tape, sticky compounds, or anything else. Hopefully, they will not find anything on the surface of the rim.

2.   Hand an index card to your assistant and ask if there are any sticky substances on this card. When he or she confirms that there are not, place the index card over the rim of the glass.

INDEX CARD

WATER

CUP

3. Ask your assistant to take a seat. Hold the glass and card directly over his or her head, and holding the card in place with your other hand, flip the glass upside down. Wiggle the card back and forth a couple of times— not much, just a little bit to set up a good seal.

4. Gently remove your hand from under the index card, and if everything goes well, the card and the water inside the glass will both stay in place. If not, have your assistant towel off and try the experiment again with a new index card.

5. Assuming you are successful, you can now flip the glass back and forth several times with a quick twist of the wrist, and the card and the water will stay in place until the card warps to the point where it buckles and the water falls out.

How Come, Huh?

We have about 100 miles of air pushing down on us at any given moment in time—one of the many blessings of living on a planet that has an atmosphere. All of this air creates about 14 to 15 pounds of pressure per square inch. This pushes on, over, and under everything on Earth. To bring this home put your hand on your forehead. For most kids this would be an area of 15 square inches. There is 225 pounds of air pressure pushing on your forehead alone— definitely a force to be reckoned with.

Pushy Index Cards

Back to the experiment. When you flipped the glass upside down, you were isolating the water and the bubble of air inside the glass. The combined weight of these two things is about 2 pounds. So you now have *2 pounds* of pressure *pushing down* on the index card from inside the glass, but there is *15 pounds* per square inch *pushing up* on the index card. When you think about approximately 100 pounds of air pressure pushing up against 2 pounds, it's not too hard to figure out who is going to win and why the card remains pushed up against the glass.

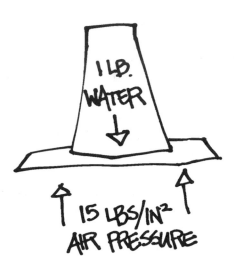

There are a couple of other factors that also help. By wiggling the card back and forth, you are creating a seal between the glass and the index card. This is due to the cohesion between water molecules— that is a whole different lab. The other factor that helps is that you are using a fairly rigid piece of material in the index card. If you try the experiment with a sheet of paper, you will get different results.

Extensions

29. Gave you one idea already. Try using a variety of different materials in place of the index card. In fact, make a list of ten different materials and see how you fare.

30. Determine if the amount of air trapped above the index card has any bearing on the experiment.

31. Different liquids, anyone?

Duel Plunger Suction

The Experiment

This experiment is a quick, easy demonstration of the ability of air to create a significant force that will keep two toilet plungers pushed together.

Materials

2   Plungers
1   Planet w/atmosphere

Procedure

1.   Place both plungers end to end so that the cups are facing one another. Grab the handles and push the plungers together, keeping them in place.

2. Once the plungers are pushed together, hold one end to create a long sword. Then grab the handles and pull the plungers apart once they are "stuck" together.

How Come, Huh?

The rubber cup on the plunger has a memory, meaning that it likes a specific shape and wants to keep that shape.

When you shove the cups together, you are evacuating the air inside the cups. As the cups expand, "remembering" their original shape, they create a region of low pressure inside the cups. The pressure outside the cups is greater than the low pressure inside, so the cups remain *pushed* together. Science never sucks.

Tap-Dancing Dimes

The Experiment

The next two labs are a pair of quick experiments that illustrate ideas on opposite ends of the spectrum. The first one deals with expanding gases that make dimes dance on bottle tops, and the second deals with contracting gases that cause bottles to indiscriminately kiss young, unsuspecting scientists on the cheek.

The tap-dancing dimes is up first and builds on the idea that air is matter and also produces a force that can be observed when this matter is heated or cooled.

Materials

1   12-oz. glass pop bottle
1   Freezer or pan of ice water
1   Pie tin with hot water
1   Dime

Procedure

1. Check the top of your bottle to make sure that it is not chipped. You will need smooth, even surfaces for this experiment to work.

2. Place the bottle in a freezer or pan with ice water for about 10 minutes.

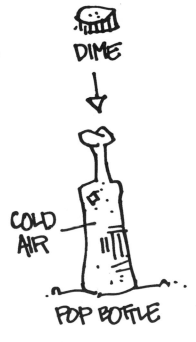

3. Take the pop bottle out of the freezer or ice water bath and place a dime squarely on the top. Do not leave any spaces where you can see down into the bottle. Place this bottle in a pie tin that has been filled with hot water. Observe the movement of the dime very carefully. If you start to quietly hum a jig, it will start to dance.

How Come, Huh?

In this experiment the air inside the bottle was cold. Cold molecules do not have as much energy, so they do not move around as much. If they don't move around as much, they take up less space so more molecules can fit inside the bottle. By cooling the bottle, you are filling it with extra molecules of air.

When you placed the cool bottle— with lots of extra molecules of air in it—into a warm water bath, you started to heat the air inside the bottle. This caused the molecules to start to have more energy, to bounce around a bit more, and to take up more room. There was more air inside the bottle than there was space for all these molecules at room temperature so the pressure inside the bottle started to increase. When it got high enough, the dime was lifted up and some of the air molecules escaped. This continued until there was a balance of forces inside and out of the bottle.

DIME PUSHED UP

WARM ESCAPES

COLD AIR WARMS AND EXPANDS

Extensions

32. Instead of a dime, place a rubber stopper firmly in the opening of the bottle. Make sure the bottle is very cold when you stopper it and that you place it in hot water.

33. Reverse the process and see if you can get the dime to stick to the top of the bottle so well that you can't pry it off using your fingers.

Kissing Bottles

The Experiment

The previous lab demonstrated that when cool air was heated, it would expand, causing pressure to build up inside a bottle covered by a dime.

We reverse the process in this experiment. Instead of cooling the bottle, then heating it, we are heating the bottle then allowing it to cool next to a soft, pliable surface—no lip gloss necessary.

Materials

1   12-oz. glass pop bottle
1   Dime
1   Microwave
    or
1   Pie tin, 9" to 12"
    Hot water

Procedure

1.   Check the top of your bottle to make sure that it is not chipped. You will need smooth, even surfaces for this experiment to work.

2.   Add a couple of drops of water to the bottle, place in the microwave, and nuke it for 30 seconds or use a pan of very hot water and leave the bottle in the water for about 3 minutes.

3.   After the bottle has had a chance to get nice and hot, place the opening of the bottle next to your cheek and leave it there for about 2 minutes. It is very important to hold the bottle very still. After the 2 minutes is up, gently pull the bottle away from your cheek. You should notice that your cheek goes with the bottle, and when you finally pull the bottle away, you will hear a smooching sound.

How Come, Huh?

The air inside the bottle was heated. When this happened, the air expanded and was forced outside the bottle. You were essentially emptying the bottle of air using heat as the driving force.

When you took the bottle out of the microwave or out of the hot water and placed the bottle next to your cheek, it started to cool. Heating the bottle removed some of the air and the bottle was also trapped against your cheek, creating a seal. As a consequence, the air pressure inside the bottle was lower than the air pressure outside in the atmosphere. With the low air pressure inside the bottle and regular air pressure inside your mouth, your cheek got pushed inside the bottle as the air inside cooled and contracted.

At some point the air inside the bottle became the same temperature as the air in the room—but there was still the matter of your cheek preventing any air from entering the bottle. As you pulled, the seal was broken and the air rushed inside the bottle to fill the space created by the low pressure. The rushing air made your cheek vibrate, which sounded like a kiss—romance without the germs.

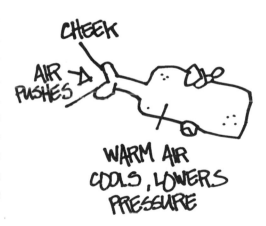

Extensions

34. Instead of a dime, place a rubber balloon inside the opening of the bottle. Make sure the bottle is very hot when you seal it with the balloon, and set it out to cool.

35. Reverse the process and see if you can get the stopper to shoot out of the bottle by placing it in the bottle when the contents are cool and then placing the bottle in very hot water.

Big Idea 5

We are completely surrounded by air and this air exerts pressure on all things. It can exert a force on matter and push it out of the way or sometimes change the shape or position of the object.

Smashing Idea...

The Experiment

...old chap. OK, the title is a really bad pun, but it gets the idea across. You can tell your friends that you can crush aluminum cans without ever touching them. You'll just use the air in the room. This is done by taking an aluminum can and heating it in the flame of a propane torch. The hot can is then inverted in a pie tin half filled with ice water. The can is crushed, literally, by the air pressure in our atmosphere.

Materials

1   Aluminum can, 12-16 ounces
1   Propane torch
1   Pair of tongs
1   Book of matches
1   9"-12" diameter pie tin
1   Cup of ice water
1   Pair of goggles
    Adult Supervision

Procedure

1. Fill the pie tin half full of water and toss in a couple of ice cubes for good measure.

2. Place a clean, empty, aluminum can—beer cans seem to work the best—in the pair of tongs. Invert it so the opening is facing down and place it in the pie tin of ice water. Let the can sit there for about 30 seconds and observe what happens, if anything.

Smashing Idea...

3. Nab the beer can in the tongs again and with the supervision of an adult, light the propane torch and heat the can for about thirty seconds, rolling it around in the flame. When the can is nice and hot, invert it so the opening is facing down and place it in the pie tin of ice water.

4. What you will notice next is very entertaining. As the air inside the can cools, the air pressure outside the can will exert a force on that can and produce a shape that is very different from the one that you started with in the first place.

How Come, Huh?

The first time you inverted the can the air pressure inside and outside the can was equal— there were no excessive forces placed on the can so there was no movement. The can retained its original shape.

When you heated the can, the air molecules inside the can started getting very excited and were bouncing around and off of each other. All this bouncing around caused the air inside the can to expand, and most of the air molecules were shoved out through the pop top opening of the can, which set the stage for the next part of the experiment.

When the can was flipped over a second time into the water, you created a closed system. No air could get in or out of the can. The air pressure outside the can pushing on the water was the same as before, but as the can cooled, the few remaining air molecules didn't take up very much space, which created low pressure inside the can.

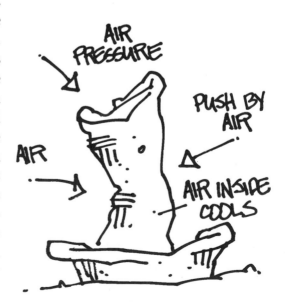

AIR PRESSURE

PUSH BY AIR

AIR

AIR INSIDE COOLS

This low pressure did not provide much resistance so the air outside collapsed the can as it pushed on it—much noisier than crushing the can against your forehead and more impressive too.

Extensions

36. This experiment works very well with one gallon metal cans with screw cap openings. Place a small amount of water inside the can, place the can on a stove. Heat the water until it is boiling then remove the can and cap it. Set the can on a level surface and allow it to cool. You will be very pleased with the results.

37. Place a rubber balloon over the end of a test tube and alternately heat and cool the tube with pans of hot and ice water.

Mashed Milk Jugs

The Experiment

This is a variation on the previous experiment, one that does not use heat but still incorporates air pressure and differences in air pressure to create change in a solid object.

An empty, clean milk jug is filled with water. A one-hole stopper with a straw trailing about 2 feet of tubing is inserted into the neck of the milk jug. The jug is inverted over the sink so that the water can run out of the jug and empty into the sink. As you watch the experiment proceed, you notice that the jug begins to collapse. Materials, please.

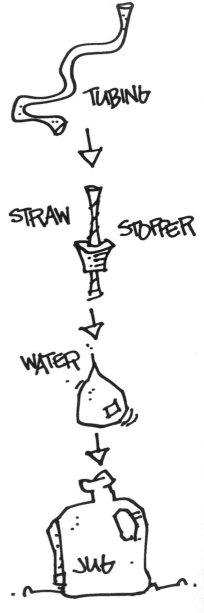

Materials

1 Plastic, gallon, milk jug
1 #3, one-hole stopper
1 2' length of tubing, 3 mm
1 1-oz. bottle of liquid soap
1 Straw
  Water
  Sink

Procedure

1. Rinse the empty milk jug with water and soap and then fill it full with clean water from the tap.

2. Insert the straw in the stopper. If you have a tough time getting the straw to slide inside, add a drop of liquid soap to the end of the straw and wiggle it in again.

3. Once the straw is inside the stopper, wiggle one end of the tubing over the other end of the straw.

4. When everything is assembled, insert the stopper in the jug and flip the whole contraption over so that water starts to empty out of the hose. If the process starts a little slow, lift the jug into the air a foot or two. Can't think of a scientific reason for why this would help, but it does sometimes.

5. Observe what happens to the shape of the milk jug.

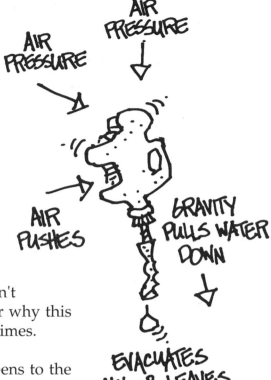

AIR PRESSURE

AIR PRESSURE

AIR PRESSURE

AIR PUSHES

GRAVITY PULLS WATER DOWN

EVACUATES JUG & LEAVES VACUUM

How Come, Huh?

When you put the stopper in the jug and flipped it over full of water, you were creating another closed system. As the water from the jug was pulled downward by gravity, there was nothing to replace it inside the jug. This reduced the air pressure inside the jug, causing the sides to collapse under the weight of the air in the room.

Extensions

38. Use this experiment to explain why submarines can be crushed by the weight of the water around them if they dive too deep or lose power and drift to the ocean floor.

39. Scuba divers sometimes get what are called the "bends." It is a very dangerous condition created by rising to the surface of the ocean too fast after a very deep dive. Explain what happens next.

The Mechanical Mosquito

The Experiment

This is an extension of the aluminum can lab that you just did, but we are going to use a material that does not crush. A pyrex test tube fitted with a stopper holding a piece of glass tubing and decorated to look like a big mosquito is dipped into a glass of blood-red liquid. Nothing happens.

The fanny of this same "mosquito" is heated in a propane flame. When the proboscis of the "mosquito" is inverted into the same cup of blood-red liquid and it is instructed to take a drink, the tube fills rapidly with the red liquid.

Materials

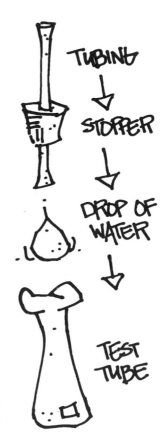

1   Pyrex test tube, 20 x 150
1   #1, one-hole stopper
1   8" piece of 3 mm glass tubing
1   Propane torch
2   Test tube clamps
1   Book of matches
1   Cup with water
1   Bottle of liquid soap
1   Pair of goggles
1   Bottle of white glue
1   Bottle of red food coloring
1   Bottle of blue food coloring
2   "Eyes" from a craft store
    Masking tape
    Adult Supervision

Procedure

1. The first thing you are going to want to do is build your mosquito. Insert the glass tubing one-third of the way into the stopper. If you have a tough time getting it into the stopper, add a dab of liquid soap to the end you are inserting.

2. When the glass tubing is inserted in the stopper, glue two eyes to the front of the stopper. Lastly, clip the two test tube clamps on to the tube so that they look like wings. Use the illustration to the right as a guide. Your mosquito is ready to perform.

3. To make your "blood," fill the cup with water and add several drops of red food coloring. To darken your blood and give it a deeper, more realistic color add blue food coloring a drop at a time. If you are doing this as a demonstration for your friends, you may want to label the cup "blood sample," using a piece of masking tape.

4. Add a drop of water to the bottom of the Pyrex test tube. This accelerates the rate of the experiment and also gives you an easy measure of when to invert the tube into the liquid. Flip the mosquito upside down in the "blood" and instruct it to drink. When nothing happens, tell your friends that sometimes you have to "encourage" the mosquito to drink, so you are going to heat its fanny.

5. Put on your goggles, and with the supervision of an adult, light the propane torch and heat the bottom of the tube. You placed a drop of water in the tube so keep an eye on that drop. When it boils and produces steam, the mosquito is ready to drink the blood. Invert the tube and stick the glass tubing in the sample of "blood." Observe what happens.

The Mechanical Mosquito

Data & Observations

In the spaces provided below draw a picture of what happened when the mosquito was given a drink of blood before and after its bottom was heated.

How Come, Huh?

The first time you inverted the tube, the air pressure inside and outside the tube was equal so there was no movement. As you heated the tube, the air molecules inside the tube started getting very excited and were bouncing around and off of each other. This heating caused the air inside the tube to expand and quite a few of the air molecules actually left the tube— very similar to the aluminum can experiment.

When the tube is flipped over a second time and the glass tube is inserted in water, you created a closed system. Nothing could get in or out of the tube. The air pressure outside the tube pushing on the water was the same as before, but as the tube cooled, the few remaining air molecules didn't take up very much space, which created low pressure inside the tube.

This low pressure does not provide much resistance so the air outside **pushes** the water up into the tube. As you can see from the amount of water that is allowed inside the tube, there was very little air left inside after the heating.

Differences in air pressure are responsible for winds being created, huge storm systems being formed, and entertaining physics experiments.

Extensions

40. Experiment with the diameter of the tube and see if there is a difference in the way the experiment comes to life. In particular, does the diameter of the mosquito's proboscis make it easier or harder to drink the blood as the diameter gets wider.

41. Set up an experiment to see if the volume of the mosquito's fanny makes a difference. You started with a Pyrex™ tube. What happens if you use a larger tube? How about a smaller one? Change the shape of the tube by substituting an Ehlenmeyer flask or maybe a boiling flask? Confused? Check the dictionary, the Internet, or poke your local chemistry teacher in the ribs.

The Water Pump

The Experiment

This is a classic experiment in air pressure circles and also doubles as a fun magic trick that you can show your friends. Challenge them to pick up the dime without getting their fingers wet. They cannot move the dime, the pie tin, or wait until the water evaporates.

To set this experiment/magic trick up, a dime is placed in a pie tin that has about a quarter of an inch of water in it. For those of you paying attention, the dime is now officially underwater. A candle is placed next to the dime, lit, and a drinking glass is placed over the candle with the edge of the glass resting on the dime. When the candle consumes all of the air inside the glass, the dime will be exposed to the air and easy to pick up without getting your fingers wet. Here's how.

Materials

1   Aluminum pie tin
1   Votive candle
1   Book of matches
1   Drinking glass, 12 to 16 oz., clear
1   Dime
    Water
1   Pair of goggles
    Adult Supervision

Procedure

1. Fill the pie tin with a quarter of an inch of water and toss the dime near the middle.

2. Place a votive candle next to the dime. Light the candle or, if your parents prefer, have an adult light the candle.

3. Place the drinking glass over the candle so that the edge of the glass rests on the dime. Observe what happens.

4. When the water is inside the glass, you can reach down and gently remove the dime from under the edge of the glass and the water should remain inside the glass. Here's why.

How Come, Huh?

By placing the glass upside down over the candle you were creating another closed system. The candle had a very limited amount of air to burn, only the gases trapped inside the glass. As the air was burned, it was removed from the inside of the glass as a bouncy, space-pigging gas and fixed to the wick of the candle as a very space-conservative, compact solid. That's one of the reasons the wick turns black.

The other thing that happens is that once the air is removed as a gas, the gas pressure inside the glass is lowered. Which makes sense—you take some of the air away and there is less air to push and create pressure. Low air pressure inside the glass, regular air pressure outside the glass creates an imbalance. There is more pressure outside the glass on the water than inside the glass on the water so the water gets pushed into the glass. The dime simply serves as a stopper to hold the "door" under the glass open so it is easier for the water outside to get pushed in. Another mystery from the world of magic revealed.

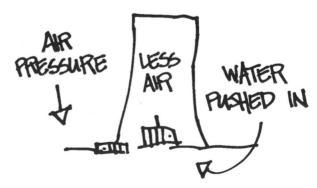

Extensions

42. Vary the size of the glass, the size of the candle, and the amount of water.

The Bashful Balloon

The Experiment

This particular experiment demonstrates several ideas. First of all it reinforces the idea that air is matter and matter takes up space. Second, if there a is difference in air pressure, that difference is sometimes great enough to create a significant amount of force. Third, not only does nature abhore a vacuum, but trying to work against one is a pain in the fanny.

Materials

1   Rubber balloon, round
2   Paper towels
1   1 gallon, widemouthed jar
1   Book of matches
1   Drinking straw
1   Pair of goggles
    Water
    Adult supervision

Procedure

1. Make a water balloon that is about twice the size of the opening of the mouth of the jar and tie it off. It should be the size of a very large grapefruit.

2. Place the jar on a hard, level surface and put the water balloon in the mouth of the jar. It should be quite a bit larger than the opening of the jar. Now, push down on the balloon from the top, try your best to shove the balloon into the jar. You may not squeeze the balloon or wiggle it down in by pushing on the sides, just push from the top.

You should notice that this is a bit tough, and despite your best efforts, the balloon simply squishes out to the sides.

3. Put on your goggles and with the supervision of an adult, remove the balloon, light a paper towel on fire with the matches, and drop it inside the jar. When you are sure that it is burning well, replace the water balloon on the opening of the jar. The balloon may bounce up and down a couple of times and then will definitely disappear into the jar. Congratulations, you have just created a water balloon vacuum.

WATER BALLOON

BURNING PAPER

GALLON JAR

4. Now try to pull the balloon out of the jar. Grab the knot that you tied and pull straight up. If you have trouble, you are in good company. Kids all over the world have tried this, and they were unsuccessful. In fact, if you are careful, you can lift the balloon up and the jar will come with it. Use caution when you do this.

5. To get the balloon out of the jar, take a straw and hold it inside the jar next to the edge of the mouth of the jar. Using your other hand, pull the balloon up to the mouth trapping the straw against the side of the jar. To remove the balloon simply give it a quick tug, and the balloon and the straw will both pop up out of the jar.

The Bashful Balloon

How Come, Huh?

The explanations for each part of the lab are described below.

A. When you placed the balloon on the mouth of the jar, you were trapping a jar full of air. Air is matter and takes up space. As you pushed on the balloon, it wouldn't go into the jar because the air in the jar was pushing back up on the balloon: There was no room for the balloon. The jar was full. As you pushed, the air inside the jar compressed slightly but not enough to allow the balloon to enter the jar.

This is another demonstration that there is air and air does take up space, which is illustrated by the cartoon to the right. You can see that the force on top of the bottle balances out the force inside the bottle created by the air. The end result is no movement.

B. When you placed the burning paper into the jar, two different opposing actions began to take place. First, the fire began to heat the air inside, which caused it to expand. These expanding air molecules created pressure inside the bottle that was not there earlier. The molecules didn't like this, so they tried to find a way out of the jar. Fortunately the balloon was resting on the top of the jar and was acting like a one-way valve. As the air continued to heat and expand, the pressure inside the jar continued to build up until it was strong enough to push the balloon up. This is like opening a valve just enough to let out a burp of air from inside the jar. Once the air escaped, the pressure was lowered inside so that the balloon once again sealed off the container. This pushing action can occur several times in rapid succession in a very short period of time. This makes the balloon look like it is dancing on top of the jar.

The other thing that is going on is the oxidation or burning of oxygen. As the paper towel burned inside the jar, the oxygen in it was changed from a gas state to a solid state. Solids take up much less space than gases, about 1800 times less, and this means that the pressure inside the jar was reduced. Low pressure inside, higher pressure outside, and the balloon got pushed into the jar. Use the illustration on page 94 to help you out if you are stuck understanding this idea. Whatever you do, remember that the balloon was pushed into the jar and not sucked.

C. In the last portion of the experiment when you were trying to get the balloon back out of the jar, you had air pressure working against you. As you pulled the balloon to the top of the jar, the air inside the jar was once again trapped behind the balloon, just like when you put the balloon on the top of the jar. The moment this happened, there was a balance of forces both inside and out. The air pressure inside the jar was equal to the air pressure outside the jar. The balloon liked this and was not going to go anywhere when this occured. If you tried to pull the balloon up, you began to create lower pressure inside the jar, and the balloon was pushed back inside by the atmosphere. When you inserted the straw, you allowed air to rush by the balloon and down into the jar to replace the

BALLOON ACTS LIKE VALVE

HOT AIR ESCAPES

AIR HEATED, EXPANDS.

The Bashful Balloon

space left by the balloon as it was being pulled up and out of the jar. If the air can get into the jar through the straw, the forces never get a chance to balance, and the balloon can be pulled from the jar very easily.

This is just an extension of the Persnickety Stopper and Uninflatable Balloon ideas that you explored earlier. If air gets trapped, it is very stubborn; if it is allowed to move from place to place, it is quite fluid, not to mention, cooperative.

Extensions

43. The classic alternative to this experiment is the egg in the milk bottle demo. Same idea, simply substitute a hard-boiled, peeled egg and a narrow-mouthed milk bottle for the water balloon and one gallon jar.

Big Idea 6

Air produces friction against moving objects. This increased friction decreases the speed that the object would otherwise fall.

Parachutes

The Experiment

A parachute is an excellent way to demonstrate the effect of air pushing against a surface, in this case a piece of fabric, to reduce the speed of a falling object.

Materials

1   Fabric handkerchief
4   Rubber bands, small
1   Spool of thread
1   Pair of scissors
1   Army soldier, toy
1   Roll of tape
1   Slingshot (optional)

Procedure

1. Cut four pieces of thread from the spool. They should each be the same length, 12 to 16 inches long.

2. Lay the handkerchief out flat and place one end of a thread on the corner. Fold the corner of the handkerchief up over the thread, and using the rubber band, bind the thread into the corner of the handkerchief. Repeat with the other three corners.

3. Take the four loose ends and bring them together. Using a small piece of tape, tape the ends into a single lump.

4. Tape the lump between the shoulder blades of the toy soldier.

5. Gently fold the handkerchief in half three times and then roll the square into a cylindrical shape so that it hugs the back of the toy soldier.

6. If you have a slingshot, place the soldier and his parachute in the slingshot and let it rip. If you are slingshotless, give the whole package a good toss in the vertical direction and hope for as much height as possible.

How Come, Huh?

The soldier used the energy that you or the slingshot gave it, until it reached its apex (top) of flight. As the soldier fell, the parachute unfolded until the heavy mass of the soldier caused it to unwind and open. Once open, the parachute pushed against the air in the atmosphere, which slowed its descent.

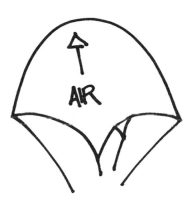

Extensions

44. Design an experiment that finds the threshold between the fixed surface area of a parachute and differing masses.

Maple Seed Flyer

The Experiment

There is a terribly creative toy company in California called the William Mark Corporation. Not only did they invent the X-zylo™, which we will detail later in the book, that sent aerodynamic engineers as well as physicists scrambling for an explanation, but they've also stolen an idea directly from the Chief upstairs.

Mark Forti, one of the founders of the company, noticed that maple trees produce seeds, called samaras, that spin to the ground like one-sided helicopters. He measured, weighed, and produced an exact replica of the maple seed on a grand scale.

Materials

1   Maple seed flyer
1   Maple seed launcher
1   Field with lots of open space

Procedure

1. Maple trees have the luxury of being able to synthesize and then drop their maple seeds from a tree branch. You are in a different position.

2. Find the launcher. It looks like a stick with a thick, durable rubber band attached to the top end. You will notice a notch where the maple seed flyer attaches to the rubber band. Hook it on to the seed and pull it back.

3. Release the maple seed flyer and you will notice that it ascends to a specific height and then stops and starts to twirl to the ground.

How Come, Huh?

When you pulled the rubber band back, you were storing energy in the elastic. When you released the flyer from your fingertips, the rubber band passed its energy to the flyer, which shot into the air, fat end first.

As gravity tugged on the flyer and air friction worked to slow it down, it eventually reached its peak, or apex, of flight and started down again. Being a one-sided design the unbalanced forces of air caused the mass to spin as it fell. The spin slowed the flyer and helped to cushion the fall.

Extensions

45. Find an actual maple leaf seed and compare the measurements—length, width, height, and mass—to the model that you have been shooting. Determine what changes, if any, had to be made by the company from the original design to get it to fly.

46. Determine if the distance that you stretch the rubber band before you release it has any effect on the height of the flyer or the number of rotations that pass before it hits the ground.

Helicopters

The Experiment

You will cut a piece of paper and fold it into a design that twirls to the ground like a helicopter. After the initial ooh aah, you can then very easily take this idea and produce a myriad of variations on this basic design. Some of these are bound to create a visual relationship for the idea that air friction slows some objects down as they fall to the Earth.

Materials

1   Pair of scissors
1   Piece of paper
1   Chair
1   Atmosphere

Procedure

1. If you must, use the pattern to the right as a template and make a pattern. Cut the design out along the perimeter, and save the extra paper for additional ideas.

2. The next cut to make is along the dashed lines. Once these cuts are made, fold one of the long strips (A) to the left, crease it along the solid line and the other (B) to the right. These are the rotors of the helicopter, and at this point it should look like a giant capital *I* with bunny ears.

3. Once these are made, fold the sides (C & D) into the middle just like you would fold a legal letter. This is the body of the helicopter.

4. The last thing to do is to fold the bottom (E) of the helicopter up about a half an inch. This fold helps keep everything together. A cartoon of what the final contraption should look like is pictured to the left.

5. Assume the helicopter flying position: Stand on the chair, extend the arm with the helicopter into the air and place your other hand on your hip. Drop said invention from outstretched, overhead arm. Make appropriate oooh-aaah noises. If the spirit of Sir Newton is with you, it will twirl to the floor.

6. Now that the excitement has subsided, drop the helicopter again and note if the rotors (those would be the big flaps on top of the helicopter) are spinning clockwise or counterclockwise.

7. Nab the helicopter and flip the rotors to the opposite sides of the body and drop it again. Record on the next page if the rotors are spinning clockwise or counterclockwise now that they have been reversed.

8. Finally, snip two inches off the end of each rotor and drop it a third time. Determine if the rotors are spinning faster or slower than when they were longer. Record this observation on the next page in the appropriate place.

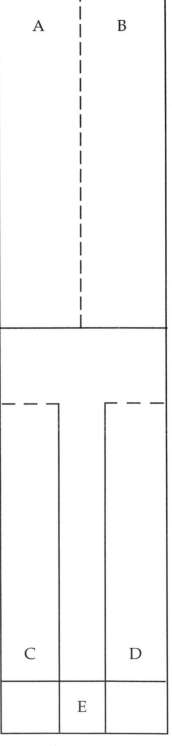

Helicopters

Data & Observations

Circle the appropriate word to describe what happened as the result of the following procedures from page 101.

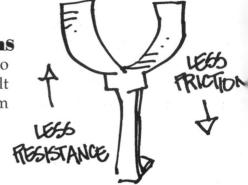

6. Clockwise

   Counterclockwise

7. Clockwise

   Counterclockwise

8. Faster

   Slower

How Come, Huh?

This is a simple exercise in air friction. As the helicopter falls to the floor, the air molecules push up against the blades and slow the descent. It spins because the blades are on opposite sides, causing unbalanced forces that spin the 'copter.

When you flip-flop the rotors, the forces are still there, but they are reversed so the helicopter spins the opposite direction. When you shorten the blades, there is less mass to push around and less friction resisting the fall, so the rotors spin faster.

Extensions

47. Adapt the design by creating a helicopter with rotors on the top and the bottom.

48. Create a helicopter that has multiple rotors on top—multiple being three or more.

Big Idea 7

The faster air moves across the surface of an object, the less pressure it puts on that surface. This is also called Bernoulli's law.

Impromptu Wing

The Experiment

A regular, old, white piece of paper is folded over a pencil forming the general shape of an airplane wing. As air travels over the top surface of the wing, it creates an area of low pressure and amazingly enough, demonstrates the principle of lift that is found in the study of Bernoulli's overarching principle of fluid dynamics that is focus of this section.

Materials

1   Pencil
1   Paper clip
1   Sheet of paper
1   Pair of scissors
1   Ruler

Procedure

1. Cut a strip of paper 3 inches wide and 11 inches long.

2. Bend the paper in half, do not fold or crease it, and paper clip the two halves of the sheet together. You can moosh the paper with your hand so it is flatter, but do not make a crease.

3. Slide the pencil into the middle of the paper so that the paper clip hangs down. Hold the "wing" up to your bottom lip and blow down on the top surface of the paper. Use the illustration to the upper right as a guide.

If the spirits of Leonardo, Orville, and Wilbur are with you, the wing will be pushed up toward your nose, and you will have now personally experienced Bernoulli's law in action.

How Come, Huh?

When you blew across the top of the wing, a difference in air pressure was created. The pressure under the wing remained constant, but the pressure over the wing was reduced. The low pressure on top of the wing allowed the pressure under the wing to push up on it. Aerodynamic engineers call this lift.

The foundation for all of this is Bernoulli's law that states that the *faster* a fluid travels *over* the surface of an object, the *less* pressure it puts on that object. Air is considered a fluid for the purposes of this experiment.

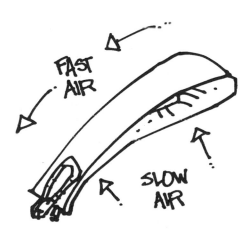

When you think about the experiment, the air under the wing was not moving at all so the pressure pushing on it remained the same. The air moving across the top of the wing was moving very fast, so it had less time to stop and push on top of the wing. When there is more pressure on the bottom of the wing than on the top, you have lift—illustration to the left.

Extensions

49. Experiment with the width and the length of the wing and prove that regardless of the changes in these two variables, the result is the same.

Collapsible Structures

The Experiment

To further develop your understanding of Bernoulli's law we are going to build a couple of different structures. The first one is a tent made out of paper, and the second is a bridge made out of paper. Both are very effective at indicating a change in air pressure.

Materials

2 Sheets of paper
1 Pair of scissors
2 Thick books
1 Set of lungs

Procedure

1. First up is the paper tent. To make the tent, fold a sheet of paper in half, hamburger bun–style. (For those of you not familiar with this tidbit of highly technical elementary science jargon, that would be a width-wise fold. A lengthwise fold is referred to as a hot dog–bun fold. Science at its finest, not to mention, most obscure.) At any rate you now have a piece of paper that has been folded in half.

2. Place the tent on the table like the picture you see above. While you press down on the sides of the tent (to keep it from blowing away), inhale and then blow gently through the opening of the tent and observe what happens to the sides of the tent as the air passes through the inside.

Probably not what you would expect to see, unless you have been paying attention to the previous labs. Record your observations in the space provide in the Data & Observations section.

3. The paper bridge is another idea that is very similar. Place two thick books about 5 inches apart.

4. Cut a sheet of paper 3 inches wide and 5 inches long. Place the paper between the two books.

5. Take a deep breath and blow under the bridge and between the books. If you have a hard time with the paper lifting and moving, put your fingers on the edges of the paper to hold it in place and try again. Record your observations in the section below.

Data & Observations

1. Circle the words that best describe what happened to the sides of the tent when you blew through the opening of the tent.

    a. No movement

    b. Collapsed inward

    c. Expanded outward

2. Circle the words that best describe what happened to the paper surface when you blew under the paper bridge.

    a. No movement

    b. Collapsed downward

    c. Expanded upward

Collapsible Structures

How Come, Huh?

When you blew through the tent and under the paper bridge, you were creating an area of fast-moving air. Once again—according to our pal, Bernoulli, the faster air travels across a surface, the less pressure it puts on that surface.

By blowing, you lowered the air pressure inside the tent as well as under the bridge. This created a difference in pressure with the other sides of the structures. We know that differences in air pressure on two surfaces of the same object create a force and that this pressure can cause movement—which is exactly what happens. The air pressure outside the tent and over the bridge is greater than the pressure inside, so it causes movement downward.

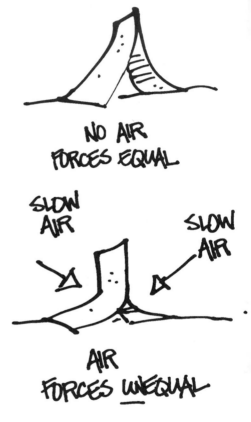

NO AIR
FORCES EQUAL

SLOW AIR

SLOW AIR

AIR
FORCES UNEQUAL

Extensions

50. Find five other situations where two flexible items are close together, the air between them can be moved, and the end result is the movement of the items. List your findings below:

1. _____
2. _____
3. _____
4. _____
5. _____

Sticky Papers

The Experiment

Another quick idea to help you with Extension 50. Two thin pieces of paper are held very near to one another. You take a deep breath and blow gently between the papers, and instead of pushing apart, they stick together. By now you should have a clue as to why.

Materials

1   Sheet of paper
1   Pair of scissors
1   Set of lungs

Procedure

1. Cut two strips of paper, 1 inch wide and 11 inches long.

2. Hold the pieces of paper directly in front of your mouth, use the illustration above as a guide, and blow between them. Observe what happens to the strips of paper.

How Come, Huh?

When you blew between the strips of paper, you were creating an area of fast-moving air. Once again, according to our pal, Bernoulli, the faster air travels across a surface, the less pressure it puts on that surface. You lowered the air pressure between these two items. This created a difference in pressure with the other sides of the structures. We also know that differences in air pressure on two surfaces of the same object create a force and that this pressure can cause move-ment—which is exactly what happens. The air pressure outside the strips of paper is greater than the pressure inside, so they came together and "stuck."

Kissin' Cousins

The Experiment

More labs that explain Bernoulli's principle. In the spirit of Extension 50 we bring you the Kissin' Cousins. A lab that probably originated in the "hollers" and canyons of Kentucky, but we'll take it strictly on its scientific merit anyway.

Two balloons are inflated and when the air pressure between them is reduced in the usual fashion, they "kiss."

Materials

2 Balloons, 9", round
2 Balloons, 9", oblong
4 18" pieces of string
1 Pair of scissors

Procedure

1. Inflate and tie off all four of the balloons. Tie one string to each balloon.

2. Hold the balloons by the string, use the cartoon above as a guide, and blow between the balloons. By now the result should be old hat, but we would like you to record your observations on the next page anyway.

3. In our desire to beat this idea to death, repeat the experiment using the oblong-shaped balloons. This robs us of one of our extension ideas, but gives you a good idea of air pressure.

Data & Observations

1. Circle the words that best describe what happened to the balloons when you blew between the round balloons.

     a. No movement

     b. Came together

     c. Pushed apart

2. Circle the words that best describe what happened to the balloons when you blew between the oblong balloons.

     a. No movement

     b. Came together

     c. Pushed apart

How Come, Huh?

When you blew between the balloons, you were creating an area of fast-moving air. According to our advisor, Bernoulli, the faster air travels across a surface, the less pressure it puts on that surface. You lowered the air pressure between these two balloons. This created a difference in pressure with the other sides of the balloons. We also know that differences in air pressure on two surfaces of the same object create a force and that this pressure can cause movement— which is exactly what happens. The air pressure outside the balloons is greater than the pressure inside, so they came together and "kissed." We are not sure if that is the proper scientific term, but it makes perfect sense to most kids.

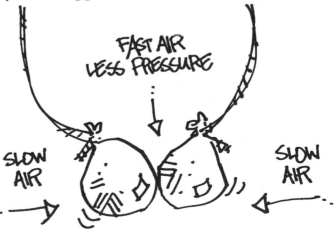

The Great Can Collision

The Experiment

Two clean, empty aluminum cans are placed about three inches apart on a bed of naked straws. Then you announce to your friends that the cans are actually magnetized and will be attracted to one another, but first you must blow an invisible barrier out of the way.

You take a deep breath, blow between the cans, and they "magically" bonk into one another. Be sure to practice this one before you demonstrate it, so that you can get the distance between the cans just right or you may pass out trying to get this one to work.

Materials

20 Large diameter, thick walled straws
 2 Empty, clean, 12 -16 oz. aluminum cans
 1 Flat, hard surface
 1 Set of lungs

Procedure

1. Take the wrappers off all of the straws. This is the naked part of the lab. Lay the straws side by side on a hard surface. They should be about a quarter to an eighth of an inch apart.

2. Place two, empty, dry cans on top of the straws about three inches apart. The lighter the can, the better; and to this end may we recommend that you take a peek at some of the beer company cans.

3. Take a deep breath and blow between the cans as hard as you can. If everything is set up properly, the cans should roll toward one another and bonk. If you are having a hard time, move the cans a little closer to one another and try again.

Data & Observations

Circle the words that best describe what happened when you blew between the aluminum cans.

    a. No movement
    b. Came together
    c. Pushed apart

The Great Can Collision

How Come, Huh?

Bernoulli's law again. When the cans are just sitting there, they are completely surrounded by air. Since all of the forces are equal, nothing is moving. When you blow between the cans, you are altering the balance of forces. The faster traveling air exerts less pressure between the cans, but the pressure on the outside of the cans remains the same. More pressure on the outside than on the inside causes the cans to move toward the center and bonk into one another.

Just for the record there is nothing magnetic or magical about this lab.

Extensions

51. This whole time we have been using our lungs to produce the air that makes all of these labs work. Time to substitute other sources of air for the lungs. Try large balloons, hair dryers, air compressors, fans, and anything else that you can think of that will produce a fast-moving stream of air. Determine if you can use these sources of air to produce the desired result.

52. If you are doing the labs in order, we started with strips of paper, then balloons, and finally cans. We asked you to find other things that would work a couple of labs back. Now that we have expanded your horizons, revisit that idea and try a pair of Ping-Pong balls.

Bernoulli Toobe

The Experiment

You and your friend each have a very long, 9 foot, plastic tube that we call a Bernoulli Toobe, thank you for forgiving our spelling idiosyncracies. You challenge your friend to a tube-inflating contest. On your mark, get set, and you smoke your buddy. Here's how . . .

Materials

2   Bernoulli Toobes
2   Sets of lungs

Procedure

Hold the opening of the Toobe up toward your mouth, but leave about six inches between you and the Toobe. Take a deep breath and blow as long and as hard as you can. What you will notice is that the Toobe will begin filling with air very rapidly. Your partner is probably holding his Toobe directly over his mouth and filling at a much slower rate.

How Come, Huh?

Bernoulli's law, of course. When you blow into the Toobe from a distance, you are lowering the air pressure at the mouth of the Toobe. This low air pressure is pushed into the tube by the higher pressure on the sides, filling the Toobe at a much faster rate than if you tried to fill the Toobe by blowing air from your lungs directly into the container.

Floating Index Cards

The Experiment

Not only can Bernoulli's law explain lift and movement, but it can also explain how and why index cards can defy gravity.

In these two experiments you are going to blow down into containers that have index cards guided by thin pieces of metal. Usually when you blow down on something it falls toward the floor, but in this case, the cards hover just under the containers.

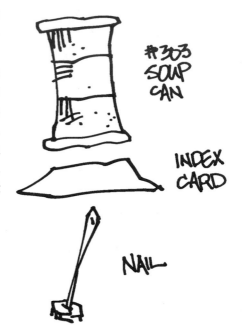

Materials

1   Soup can, # 303, empty
1   8-penny nail
1   Hammer
1   Sewing spool , empty
1   Straight pin
2   Index cards
    Adult Supervision

Procedure

1. Flip the soup can upside down on a hard surface, and using the nail, punch a hole in the middle of the bottom of the can. Wiggle the nail around so that the nail has room to move and so that it can be inserted and removed easily. Also make a hole in the center of one of the index cards using the same nail.

2. Slide the nail into the index card, snugging the head of the nail up to one side. Then insert the nail into the can. Holding the index card in place with one hand, hold the can up to your mouth with the other.

3. Blow into the can as hard as you can. Remove your hand from the index card just after you start blowing. If everything is going the way it should, the card will remain suspended next to the can as long as you can blow air into it.

4. A variation on this lab uses a sewing spool and pin. Push the straight pin into the middle of the second index card and wiggle it around a bit. Insert the pin into one end of the sewing spool. Using the same technique as you did with the soup can, blow into the other end of the spool and keep the card from falling to the ground. Use the illustration above as a guide.

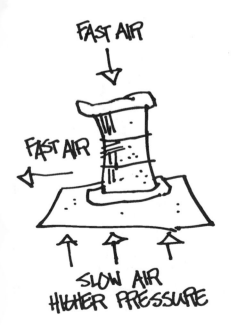

FAST AIR

FAST AIR

SLOW AIR
HIGHER PRESSURE

How Come, Huh?

The air moving through the holes was forced, at high speed, out of the containers and across the top surface of the index card. The faster a fluid moves across a surface, the less pressure it exerts on that surface. You lowered the air pressure on the top of the card. The air pressure under the card remained unchanged. More pressure on the bottom of the card than on the top of card means that it is not going to go anywhere until you run out of breath.

Funnel Frolics

The Experiment

You are going to learn two experiments that not only demonstrate Bernoulli's law, but also are a lot of fun to try on your friends. The first experiment requires that you tip your head back, place the funnel in your mouth, and place the Ping-Pong ball in the funnel. When you are ready, blow as hard as you can and try to get the Ping-Pong ball to pop out of the funnel. It won't happen. Next bend over, point the funnel to the floor, hold the ball inside the funnel and start to blow. As long as you can blow hard, the ball will not drop to the floor.

Materials

1   Funnel
1   Ping-Pong ball
1   Set of lungs

Procedure

1. Tip your head back and place the funnel in your mouth. Then place the ball in the funnel, use the illustration to the right as a guide. Take a deep breath and blow as hard as you can, try to blow the ball out of the funnel. It won't happen—we promise.

If you want to make a bet with your friends, most of them will scoff at the idea that you can't blow a wimpy little ball out of a funnel—and you will win a lot of sodas.

2. Hopefully you didn't pass out trying that last experiment. As hard as it is to imagine that you can't blow that Ping-Pong ball out of the funnel, imagine telling your friends that you can keep a ball from falling to the floor simply by blowing down on it. There's another soda on the way, guaranteed.

Put the funnel in your mouth as you look at the floor. Hold the Ping-Pong ball in the funnel and start to blow. A second after you start, remove your hand. The difference in air pressure will keep the Ping-Pong ball pushed up in to the funnel. Amazed looks all around.

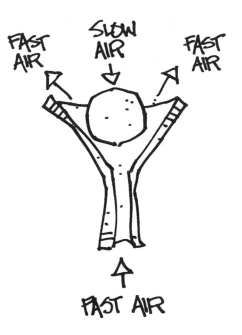

How Come, Huh?

Bernoulli's law states that the faster that air travels over the surface of an object the less pressure it will put on that object. When you blow into the funnel, the air coming out is moving very fast compared to the air in the room. As this fast-moving air travels over the bottom surface of the Ping-Pong ball, it actually reduces the pressure on the side of the ball that is nearest the opening. The other side of the ball remains unchanged, which means that we create a dramatic difference in pressure that always pushes the ball down into the funnel, and the harder you blow, the harder the ball is pushed into the funnel.

Funnel Frolics

How Come, Huh?

In idea #1 the ball is resting in the funnel. Gravity is holding it in place and you would think that a quick burst of air would pop it right out. However, when you blow into the funnel, you are reducing the pressure on the underside of the ball and actually forcing it farther into the funnel. Illustrations should help.

In idea #2 you are holding the ball in place until you can start blowing. Once the air starts traveling over the top surface of the ball, it reduces the pressure on that side, but the air pressure underneath the ball is great enough to hold it in place until you run out of breath. Weird but true and definitely good for winning a couple of bets with your pals.

FAST AIR

FAST AIR

FAST AIR

SLOW AIR

Extensions

53. We have used sewing spools to support index cards and plopped Ping-Pong balls in funnels that were upside down. Let your imagination run wild and figure out other things to put in the funnel that can be supported with a breath of air. Stumped? Try a paper disk, a partially inflated balloon. Make a list of five other things that work.

54. Rig an air compressor up to a piece of PVC tubing and see how many items can be placed at the other end of the opening to take advantage of Bernoulli's law.

Instant Atomizer

The Experiment

An atomizer is a contraption that takes fluids and disperses them into small, atom-sized packets.

In this lab you are going to adapt a regular, old, ordinary straw, so that it becomes an atomizer. The joy of science, once again at your lips.

Materials

1   Straw
1   Pair of scissors
1   Glass of water

Procedure

1. Locate the top one-third of the straw. Snip the straw two-thirds of the way through the body at this place.

2. Bend the straw to a 90-degree angle and insert the longer end in the water. Keeping the straw bent open, blow quickly through the straw and across the opening. The water in the straw will rise up and be atomized on its way across the room.

How Come, Huh?

When you blew across the split in the straw, you lowered the air pressure over the straw. The water pressure inside the straw and the air pressure pushing down on the surface of the water in the cup remained the same, so when the pressure inside the straw was lowered the water took the opportunity to rise up in the straw. As it hit the area where the cut was made, the air blowing through the straw atomized the water into tiny little droplets that shot across the room.

Anti-Gravity Ping-Pong

The Experiment

A Ping-Pong ball is placed in a concentrated stream of cool air that is blowing out of a hair dryer. When the ball is placed in the stream of air, it is pushed upward and stays suspended above the dryer. No big surprises yet. But, when you tip the dryer sideways the Ping-Pong ball will remain suspended over the floor even at angles where it would normally fall to the ground. Weird? No, Bernoulli's law in action. Gotta love science, it takes all the mystery and superstition out of living.

Materials

1   Hair dryer
1   Ping-Pong ball
1   8.5" by 11" sheet of paper
1   8" piece of masking tape

Procedure

1. Tear the masking tape into four, 2 inch pieces. Roll the sheet of paper into a tube forming a narrow cone and tape it together with two of the pieces of tape. The bottom of the cone should be just large enough to slide on to the nozzle of the hair dryer with not much room left over. Tape the cone on to the dryer nozzle with the remaining two pieces of tape.

2. Turn the hair dryer on and definitely use the cool setting if you have one. If you only have a hot air setting, the hot air eventually warps and mutates the plastic ball.

3. Once the stream of air is blowing, place the ball in the top of the cone. The ball may drop down inside the cone for a second, but it will probably pop back out. If it does not, turn the dryer off and trim a couple of inches off the top of the cone. For this experiment to work well, the ball will need to be suspended in the air column above the top of the cone where everyone can see it.

4. Gently tip the hair dryer back and forth about 10 to 15 degrees or so. Observe the movement of the ball in the air stream. See if you can tip the ball over so that it is extended out beyond the edge of the cone, use the illustration to the right as a guide. Experiment and see how far you can tip the dryer sideways before the ball falls out of the air stream and down to the floor.

PING-PONG BALL

PAPER

HAIR DRYER

5. Just for laughs, see if you can get the Ping-Pong ball to float up in the cone when you flip your design upside down. If a long cone presents you with problems at first, then try shortening it. This is taken from a previous lab, Funnel Frolics. If you have not done that lab then retreat, lab up, and try this idea again.

Anti-Gravity Ping-Pong

How Come, Huh?

When the ball was in the stream of air, the air pressure all around the middle of the ball was reduced. The fast-moving air put less pressure on that portion of the ball. However, the air directly on top of the ball as well directly underneath was not moving nearly as fast. It had more time to stop and push on the ball, so the pressure was greater in those two places.

Those two regions of higher pressure acted like axles on your bicycle, allowing the ball to spin freely but holding it in place. When you tipped the hair dryer sideways, gravity started acting on the ball, but the difference in pressure from the middle to the axis (top and bottom) of the ball kept it in place for a while. As you continued to tip the dryer, the force of gravity pulling down on the ball was greater than the forces holding the ball in place, so it dropped to the ground.

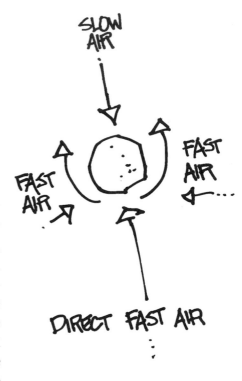

As far as the final idea, you should not have been able to get it to work. The reason the Ping-Pong ball stayed in the funnel was because there was pressure directly on top of or underneath the ball. In this case the pressure is on the sides.

Extensions

55. There are a number of other objects that can be inserted in place of the Ping-Pong ball. For starts try a small, round balloon or a ziplock baggie full of air, both weighted with a small amount of water or styrofoam packing peanuts. Let your imagination run wild.

Big Idea 8

The motion of an object can be described by its position, direction of motion, and speed.

Before You Start Folding

Making Paper Airplanes

This section of the book has the potential to be the most fun, and it also has the ability to be the most frustrating. Every plane that is in this book has been folded, flown, and perfected at my fingertips and those of my son and several of his friends. They all work, but like any puzzle, or model that you work on, each prototype has its own peculiarities. You will find that the weight of the paper that you use, the humidity in the air, and the number of stray dogs eager to play catch will all factor into the success of each plane. Be patient, don't give up easily, and if all else fails, know that you are another in a very long line of aeronautical engineers and designers who proudly bear the knowledge that they too launched a couple hundred lemons into the air.

Hot Dogs vs. Hamburgers

As we give you directions to start your airplanes, we may ask you to make either a hot dog fold or a hamburger fold. These are not food-wrapping techniques smuggled out of one of the many fast-food franchise chains our country has spawned; but they are rather simple directional folds devised by kindergarten teachers. Here they are in all their glory:

HOT DOG FOLD

HAMBURGER FOLD

A hot dog fold is a lengthwise fold, producing a long rectangle that would be suitable, if it were made from flour, salt, and yeast to hold a hot dog.

A hamburger fold is a width-wise fold that is shorter and fatter and a more likely candidate to hold a round, short, fat hamburger.

...A Couple of Tips

Making Lemonade...

You have carefully followed every direction that we gave you. You perched yourself on a chair or overlooking the entryway in your house and launched a beautifully folded airplane into the air ... only to have it wobble, nose-dive, or schnibble into the floor.

Congratulations! You have built and launched a lemon—a vehicle that does not perform particularly well. This experience may follow you into the realm of automotive or appliance purchases when you are older. Try to avoid making it a habitual part of your life.

However, as the saying goes, when life gives you lemons, make lemonade. Learn from your mistakes. Make the best of the situation. Adapt. This is the nature of invention. Try these things first, and then, if none of them helps, you may retire your creation to the circular file.

1. *Tape the wings together.*
2. *Remove the tape holding the wings together.*
3. *Emphasize the creases in your folds, especially from body to wing.*
4. *Try throwing it up at an angle of 30 to 40 degrees.*
5. *Throw it harder.*
6. *Don't throw it so hard.*
7. *Angle the wings up a bit so that the body of the plane and the wings form more of a triangle pattern.*
8. *Fold the wings down a bit.*
9. *Straighten the nose out and don't aim for the wall.*
10. *Add a paper clip to the undercarriage.*

A Basic Bomber

Step 1

Fold a regular-size sheet of
paper in half, hot dog–bun fold,
crease it, and open it again.

Step 2

Fold the upper right-hand
corner of your airplane to the
center crease.

Step 3

Fold the upper left-hand
corner of your airplane to the
center crease.

Step 4

Fold the left-hand side of the
plane over onto the right-hand
side, concealing the folds.

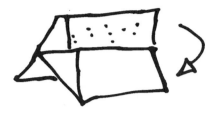

Step 5

Fold the front side of the plane straight down, halfway, to form the first wing.

Step 6

Fold the other side of the plane straight down, matching the other side, to form the other wing.

Step 7

Add three or four paper clips to the nose of the plane and throw your completed plane up and away from your body.

The Pokeyereyeout Dart

Step 1
Fold a regular-size sheet of paper in half, hot dog–bun fold, crease it, and open it again.

Step 2
Fold the upper right-hand corner of your airplane to the center crease.

Step 3
Fold the upper left-hand corner of your airplane to the center crease.

Step 4
Fold the right-hand corner of your airplane to the center crease.

Step 5
Fold the left-hand corner of your airplane to the center crease

Step 6
Fold the left-hand side of the plane over onto the right-hand side, concealing the folds.

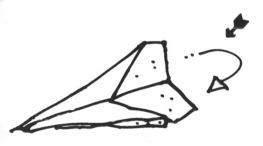

Step 7
Fold the top edge of the wing down to match the bottom edge of the body. Repeat on the other side to make a matching wing.

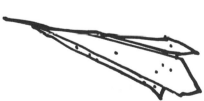

Step 8
Throw your completed plane up and away from your body at a 30-degree angle. Watch for eyes.

Le Concorde

Step 1

Fold a regular-size sheet of
paper in half, hot dog–bun fold,
crease it, and open it again.

Step 2

Fold the upper right-hand
corner of your airplane to the
center crease.

Step 3

Fold the upper left-hand
corner of your airplane to the
center crease.

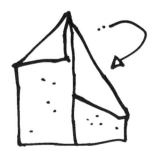

Step 4

Fold the right-hand corner
of your airplane to the center
crease.

Step 5
Fold the left-hand corner
of your airplane to the center
crease

Step 6
Fold the left-hand side of the
plane over onto the right-hand
side, concealing the folds.

Step 7
Fold the top edge of the wing
straight down leaving a one-
inch body. Repeat on the other
side to make a matching wing.

FRONT VIEW

Step 8
Add a one-inch flap on the back
of each wing and experiment
with flying the plane flaps up
and flaps down.

Long-Distance Glider

Step 1

Fold a regular-size sheet of paper in half, hot dog–bun style, crease it, and open it to full size again.

Step 2

Fold the upper right-hand corner of your airplane to the center crease.

Step 3

Fold the upper left-hand corner of your airplane to the center crease.

Step 4

Fold the point of your plane down to center crease, making a rectangle.

Step 5

Fold the upper right-hand corner of your airplane to the center crease.

Step 6

Fold the upper left-hand corner of your airplane to the center crease.

Step 7

Fold the center tip up so that it covers and holds the base of the two flaps that you just folded.

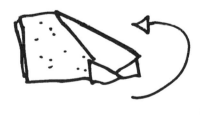

Step 8

Fold the left-hand side of the plane over onto the right-hand side, exposing the folds.

Long-Distance Glider

Step 9

Fold the top edge of the wing down to match the bottom edge of the body.

Step 10

Flip the plane over and fold the top edge of the other wing down to match the bottom edge of the body.

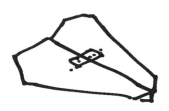

Step 11

Place a piece of tape on top of the plane to hold the two wings together.

Step 12

Throw your completed plane up and away from your body level with the floor.

The Acrobat

Step 1
Fold the upper right-hand corner down to the left edge of the paper.

Step 2
Unfold.

Step 3
Fold the upper left-hand corner down to the right edge of the paper.

Step 4
Unfold.

The Acrobat

Step 5

Tuck the center of each previous fold into the middle and form a triangle like the picture above.

Step 6

Fold the top of the triangle down until it touches the base of the triangle.

Step 7

Fold the left-hand side of the plane over onto the right-hand side, concealing the folds.

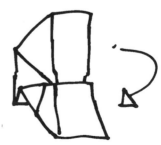

Step 8

To make the first wing fold the edge straight down leaving about an inch for the body of the plane.

Step 9
Fold the other side to match the first, creating the second wing.

Step 10
Open the plane an allow the folds to relax.

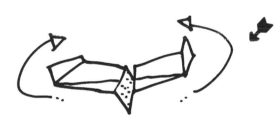

Step 11
Fold one side of each wing up to provide more stability.

Step 12
Add a one-inch flap on the back of each wing and experiment with flying the plane flaps up and flaps down.

A Cambered Wing

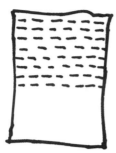

Step 1

Start with a regular-size sheet of paper and mark half-inch marks five-eighths of the way down the sheet.

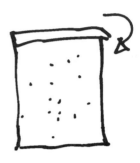

Step 2

Fold the top half-inch down and give it a good crease.

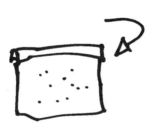

Step 3

Continue folding the top edge of the plane down in half-inch sections until you reach the five-eighths mark.

Step 4

Place a piece of tape to hold the folds in place.

Step 5

Gently mold the shape of the wing into a wide U by sliding it over the edge of a table.

Step 6

Shape the wing so that it slopes upward gently.

Step 7

Hold the wing between your thumb and forefinger and starting at your chest push the wing away from and out into its flight pattern.

Porter's Shuttle

Step 1

Fold a regular-size sheet of paper in half, hot dog–bun style, crease it, and open it to full size again.

Step 2

Fold the upper right-hand corner of your airplane to the center crease.

Step 3

Fold the upper left-hand corner of your airplane to the center crease.

Step 4

Fold the point of your plane down to center crease, making a rectangle.

Step 5
Fold the top 2 inches of the plane down

Step 6
Flip the plane over and rotate it 90 degrees counterclockwise.

Step 7
Fold the bottom half of the plane up so that it matches the top edge. Your plane is exactly one half the size in Step 6.

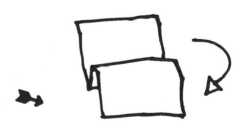

Step 8
Fold the front side of the wing down, leave about 1 inch for the body of the plane.

Porter's Shuttle

Step 9

Fold the other wing down to match the first one that you folded.

Step 10

Flip the plane over and fold the top edge of the other wing down to match the bottom edge of the body.

Step 11

Huck that baby.

Two Loops

The Experiment

Now that you have mastered airplanes and have a pretty good idea of how Bernoulli's law contributes to flight we are going to venture into the realm of the partially explained. You are going to build a glider that consists solely of two loops attached to the opposite ends of a straw. If you toss it with the large loop first, it falls almost immediately to the ground. However, if you toss it with the small end first, it will glide up to a 100 feet or more. How does it work? That's a very good question.

Materials

2   1.5" by 11" strips of paper
1   Plastic straw
1   Pair of scissors
1   8" piece of masking tape

Procedure

1. Using the the pair of scissors, cut one of the 11-inch strips to 5 inches and the other to 8 inches.

2. Tear the 8-inch piece of masking into 4 separate 2-inch pieces and hang them on the edge of the table where it will be convenient to get to them.

3. Place a piece of tape on the top edge of the larger of the two strips of paper. The illustration shows you where it should go. Roll that strip of paper into a loop and tape it together. Do the same thing with the smaller strip of paper. When you are done you will have two loops, one a little bit larger than the other.

Two Loops

4. If your straw has a wrapper on it, it is now time to undress it so that we have naked plastic. Place a piece of tape across one end of the straw forming a capital *T*.

5. Flip the straw over and put the last piece of tape over the other end forming a capital *I*, or, as was pointed out to me by a very astute student one time, a fat *H* if you turn it sideways.

6. Hold the straw perpendicular to the floor and slide the larger of the two loops over one end of the straw. Using the tape on the straw, fix the loop to that end of the straw.

7. Repeat this on the other end of the straw with the smaller loop. Your plane is now complete and should look something like the illustration below.

8. It is now time to experiment. Try the following things and record the results in the data table provided below.

    a. Toss your glider, large loop first.
    b. Toss your glider, small loop first.
    c. Toss your glider, small loop first, parallel to the floor.
    d. Toss your glider, small loop first, up at a 45° angle.
    e. Replace the front loop with one that is smaller and repeat trial b, above.
    f. Add a third loop anywhere you would like and compare the flight of that plane to all of the others.

Data & Observations

Time to put instruction number 8 to work. Using each of the six suggestions listed in that instruction, toss the glider and evaluate the flight based on the criteria listed in the data table. Place an *x* in the appropriate box based on how you feel the glider flew.

Trial	Try Again	Not Bad	Wow	Clinic Time!
a				
b				
c				
d				
e				
f				

Two Loops

How Come, Huh?

This is one of those fun ones where no one has really figured it out yet, so what you are about to read is simply an educated guess and has not been definitively proven. By the way, both bumblebees and helicopters fall into this category as well. Based on the mathematical models that we have and the laws of physics that we have discovered, neither of those two things are supposed to be able to fly— bad news for bumblebee self-esteem if they ever learn to read.

As you toss the glider, you are giving it energy to overcome the pull of gravity. When the glider leaves your hand, it starts to travel through the air, and as you know, air is matter that takes up space and also creates friction. As a result of these two things, it also has the ability to create different amounts of pressure on and around flying objects. Nothing new so far.

As the glider starts to travel through the air, there is a center of pressure created inside the front loop that pushes up on that ring. How this happens I have no idea. The front loop also creates a current of air that not only flows through but around the front ring. The larger loop at the back of the glider, following in the wake of the front loop, acts as a stabilizer and rechannels that current of air, which also creates a center of pressure that continues to push up on the glider. The air also creates friction that gradually slows the glider down. When the potential energy that you gave the glider as you tossed it is used up, the plane eventually loses the battle to gravity and winds up on the floor. We call that an educated guess. The ball is now in your court.

Extensions

56. Experiment with changing the length of the straw. Some candy stores sell huge 3-foot straws full of a sour-tasting powder. If this sounds familiar, nab one and make an albatross-sized glider.

57. Add loops to the plane in a variety of locations.

58. Change the shape and position of the loops.

Big Idea 9

Newton's First Law. An object at rest, or in equilibrium, will remain in that state unless a force acts on that object to change its speed, shape, or direction of movement.

Gyros

The Experiment

OK, you're thinking, "A gyro doesn't fly, why is it in this book?" The motion of a gyroscope is going to help explain how two flying objects zip through the air.

A gyroscope is a spinning wheel usually mounted in a movable frame. Two common examples of gyros are bicycle wheels and spinning tops. Both stand up straight when they are spinning, and both tend to fall toward the earth when they are stopped. Gravity-defying gizmos, that's what gyros are.

Materials

1   Gyro with stand
1   18" Length of cotton string
1   Fellow scientist

Procedure

1. First a little gyroscope anatomy. Review the drawing to the right so that you are familiar with the different parts of the gyroscope.

2. Place the stationary gyroscope in its stand with the axle straight up and down. Let go and see what happens to the gyro.

3. Wind the string around the axle, give it a tug, and when the gyro is spinning, try to balance it on the stand. Observe what happens to the gyro as it spins.

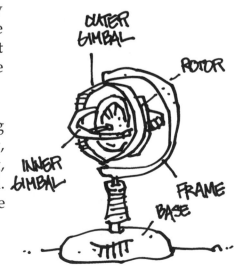

OUTER
GIMBAL

ROTOR

INNER
GIMBAL

FRAME

BASE

4. Get the gyro spinning as fast you can and balance it on the tip of your finger. With your other hand, gently push down on the top end of the axle and observe what happens.

5. Once again, get the gyroscope spinning quickly and balance it on the piece of string that you and your partner have stretched between you. Place the gyroscope on the string so that it is parallel to the ground. Observe what happens.

How Come, Huh?

When the gyroscope is spinning it has angular momentum, which is described by the equation, $H=MR^2W$. M is the mass of the spinning object, R is the radius of the wheel squared, and W is the velocity of the spin. What this equation tells us, in a nutshell, is that a large, heavy wheel that is spinning very fast has a bucket load of energy that we call angular momentum.

This energy opposes or fights against the pull of gravity. Why? The spinning motion also creates a centrifugal force, the same force that keeps water from falling out of a spinning bucket. So a spinning gyroscope can be placed on a fingertip, string, or any other stand and it will continue to stay in place as long as it is spinning and producing angular momentum and centrifugal force.

Flying Coffee Can Lids

The Experiment

We aren't exactly sure, but urban legend has it that the great granddaddy of the modern-day Frisbee™ was a plastic lid off a coffee can. If you skipped the section on gyros, you will want to go back so you understand this lab better. If you are doing these in sequence, then you're good to go.

We defined a spinning ring as a gyro. We can extend this definition if the ring is solid. A flying disc moves through the air in a stable and predictable fashion because it is subject to the same forces, angular momentum and centrifugal force, as a gyro.

Materials

1   Plastic, circular lid
1   Frisbee™
1   Fellow scientist or
    Cooperative dog
    Open area

Procedure

1. Take your Frisbee™ or similar knockoff and your plastic lid out into a large, open space. Compare the weight of the two discs and pay special attention to where the weight is located.

2. To toss the disc hold it under the edge with your four fingers, trapping the top of the disc in place with your thumb. Bring the disc across your body and toss it away from your chest, snapping your wrist at the end of the motion— kind of like a whip.

3. When you get comfortable throwing the disc, toss each disc across the field to your partner or dog and notice the length of the flight, the stability of the flight, and anything else that stands out.

4. Now toss the two discs, but do it without spinning them as you throw.

5. Hold the disc upside down and give it toss. Compare the flight starting in this position with the others.

How Come, Huh?

When the discs are spinning, they also have angular momentum that, as we know from the previous lab, is described by the equation, $H=MR^2W$. Again, what this equation tells us is that the larger and heavier that the spinning disc is, the more stable and predictable its flight will be.

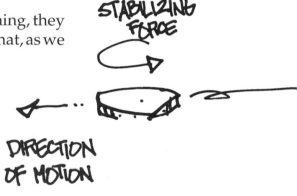

The reason for this is that the edge of the disc is weighted—particularly with the Frisbee™. When you toss the disc, you give it energy that starts the disc moving in two directions, 1) away from you and 2) in a circular motion. The first force propels the disc out into the field, the second force allows the disc to travel in a stable and predictable manner due to the angular momentum.

Extensions

60. Experiment by adding weight to the perimeter of the plastic lid. According to our formula as the weight increases the stability of the flight path should also increase. True?

61. Try three different plastic lids that have different diameters, but due to some rigging on your part, all weigh the same amount. Does the radius contribute to the stability?

Flying Soda Cans

The Experiment

Sounds like one of the scenes from *Animal House* that wound up on the cutting room floor. Actually, you can fly all kinds of cans, something that you will find out, but lightweight beer and soda cans seem to produce the best results.

Materials

1	Pair of tin snips
1	Pair of pliers
3-5	Cans, empty

Procedure

1. Make sure that your cans are empty, clean, and dry. Remove both ends.

2. Using the illustrations to the far right, on the next page prepare three different cans.

A. The first one is cut in half and the top edge of the can is even.

B. The second one starts out the same height as the first, but as you cut the can down, cut at an angle so that it looks like the picture to the right.

C. And finally, start with a half a can and cut a wave pattern into the top edge. This design is the one that most resembles a flying toy called an X-zylo, which we will introduce to you next.

3. Time to toss the cans. Using that same technique that produces a nice, tight spiral in the game of football, bring the cans back to your ear and hold your elbow perpendicular to your body. Quickly drop your elbow to your side and spin the can off your fingertips.

If everything goes according to Hoyle, the can will leave your hand and start flying down the hallway.

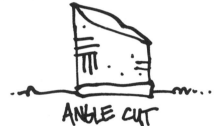

EVEN CUT

4. Once you have tried the three designs that we suggest, start hunting around see if you can find other types of containers—they do not necessarily have to be metal—and try them out.

ANGLE CUT

How Come, Huh?

The rim of the can is weighted. As soon as you start that rim spinning the centrifugal force acts like a gyro and stabilizes the can.

The air flowing through and outside the can behaves like it is flowing over a wing, which actually it is, and the

WAVE CUT

center of pressure inside the can generates lift. The upshot of all this is that the combination of the two forces, center of pressure and the gyroscopic motion, work together to allow the cans to fly.

The different wing shapes allow you to experiment with the effects of turbulence that occur as the can flies through the air. The different wing designs create different disturbance patterns, and as a result, different distances.

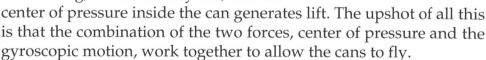

The X-zylo

The Experiment

The culmination of this section is a relatively new flying toy called the X-zylo. It was invented in 1991 by Mark Forti who was an engineering student at Baylor University in Texas at the time.

The X-zylo consists of a ring or gyroscope and wing. It weighs less than one ounce (25 grams) and has been thrown 218 yards, over 655 feet. Never before has something so light been thrown so far.

Materials

1   X-zylo
1   Large, open area
1   Fellow scientist

Procedure

1. It will take just a little bit of practice to learn how to throw the X-zylo, but once you get the hang of it, you will be able to toss it the length of a football field or more.

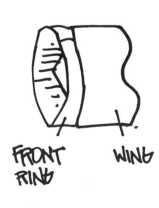

FRONT RING   WING

2. You will notice that one side of the X-zylo has a rigid, stiff ring. This is the front edge of the X-zylo. Locate the seam where the X-zylo is glued on to itself. This is the place where it should be gripped with your middle and index fingers

3. Using that same technique that produces a nice, tight spiral in the game of football, bring the X-zylo back to your ear and hold your elbow perpendicular to your body.

Quickly drop your elbow to your side and spin the X-zylo off your fingertips. Unlike football, you do not need to launch the X-zylo up at a 30-degree angle to get good distance. Instead, toss it as fast and as hard as you can, throwing it down and to the left a bit if you are right-handed, and down and to the right a bit if you are left-handed.

You will notice that the X-zylo spins rapidly and drops for a fraction of a second until it starts to gain altitude and takes off down the field. Perfection!

4. Before we get into the hows and whys of flight, we would like you to try the following experimental flights with your X-zylo and your partner. Make sure that you toss the X-zylo several times for each suggestion to get a good idea of how it behaves in flight.

a. Try tossing it backwards, with the lighter wing leading the way. Make a mental note of the flight.

b. Try tossing the X-zylo, but do it without having it spin. Record the stability, distance, and predictability of the flight.

c. Now toss the X-zylo again, throwing it for distance according to the first set of directions you received. Compare the distance, path of flight, and predictability of flight path with the other two kinds of tosses.

How Come, Huh?

So what makes this gizmo fly so well? For starters, it is a combination of the ideas that we have developed in the last two labs. But first, we need to define a couple of terms: center of gravity and center of pressure.

To find the center of gravity take a pencil and find the point on the inside of the wing where the X-zylo balances. Use the illustration to the right as a guide.

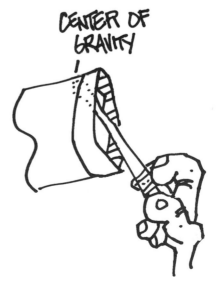

CENTER OF GRAVITY

The X-zylo

You will notice that the heavy ring in the front of the X-zylo causes the center of gravity to be more toward the edge of the ring. This is where gravity has its greatest downward effect.

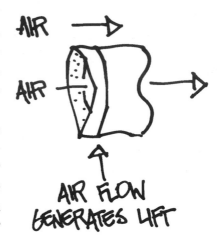

AIR FLOW GENERATES LIFT

The center of pressure is the point where most of the lifting pressure, created by the flow of air over the wing, passes. This is where the wing experiences the upward push or lift created by the difference in air pressure.

For an airplane—or any other object for that matter—to have a stable flight, the center of pressure and the center of gravity must be very near one another. If they are not, the plane will tumble due to unbalanced forces.

The fact that you have a heavy ring that shifts the center of gravity forward to match the center of pressure simply means that you are balancing the machine for flight.

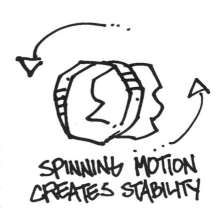

SPINNING MOTION CREATES STABILITY

OK, let's quit foolin' around and get to the meat of the subject at hand. When you toss the X-zylo, you do two things:

1. The whole thing is flying through the air because you gave it a shove. By virtue of the fact that it is flying through the air, the air is acting on the wing. This creates the lift that allows the X-zylo to fly. Now add to that the fact that,

2. You started the ring, which is actually a gyroscope, spinning. The spinning motion creates angular momentum that stabilizes the whole contraption.

So, if you step back and look at it in its simplest terms, here is the explanation, to date, that works. Start with the fact that aerodynamically the design is balanced. The center of pressure is over the center of gravity. So far, so good. By throwing the X-zylo you start the air flowing over and under the wing portion of the design, creating lift so that the design can fly. At the same time you started the gyroscope spinning; this stabilized the leading edge of the design, keeping it upright and flying in a relatively straight direction. There you have it— balance, lift, and a stabilizer.

Big Idea 10

Newton's Second Law. Force equals mass times acceleration. Or, the bigger it is and the faster it goes, the more it hurts when it hits.

Rocket on a String

The Experiment

Newton's Second Law: A law of physics that we see in sporting events and NASCAR™ racing all the time. The formula for the law is written as F=ma, or, Force equals mass times acceleration. In other words, the more energy you apply to an object, the faster and farther it will go. Maximum application of this law is the object of any shot-putter, most javelin throwers, and the average second grader standing on the bank of a river with a fistful of rocks.

We are going to start our day off by experimenting with balloon rockets. These rockets will give you an idea of what Newton's second law is about.

Materials

2 Balloons
1 Straw
1 Piece of string (30 feet)
4 4" Strips of masking tape
1 Partner

Procedure

1. You will be working with a partner through all of these activities. Thread the string through the soda straw.

2. Inflate the balloon but do not tie it off. You will need the air to escape to provide the necessary thrust for your rocket. Using two pieces of masking tape attach the balloon to the straw. Use the illustration on the next page as a guide.

Rocket on a String

3. Ask your partner to walk to the other end of the room with the string. You should have the balloon in one hand, pinching the neck to hold the air in, and the end of the string in the other. Your partner should have the other end of the string.

4. When everyone is ready, the balloon holder needs to lift the balloon to chin level for launch and the partner needs to hold the other end of the string at belly-button level. You will say, "three, two, one, launch!" and when you come to the word, "launch," let go of your balloon, allowing the air to escape, which pushes the balloon forward.

5. After you have completed your flight, work with your partner to fill in the data table. You will launch and record the amount of time it takes for your balloon to travel to the end of the string three times. Average those times and enter that information in the data table.

6. Add a second balloon and race it down your string three more times. Once all of the data has been entered, create a *bar* graph on page 164 showing the information. After that is complete, *infer* how fast you think a rocket with three and four "engines" would travel by drawing bars to represent what you *think* the data would look like.

Data & Observations

Rocket	Time Measurements		
	Trial #1 (sec.)	Trial #2 (sec.)	Trial #3 (sec.)
1 Balloon Engine			
2 Balloon Engines			

	Average Times	Inferred Times
1 Balloon Engine	_____	
2 Balloon Engines	_____	
3 Balloon Engines		_____
4 Balloon Engines		_____

How Come, Huh?

As you released the neck of the balloon, air began escaping out the back— the action. For every action there is an equal and opposite reaction. In this case the air pushed against the front and sides of the balloon producing a net forward force and so the balloon propelled along the string. There is an illustration on the top of page 162 designed to give you a bit of visual insight into exactly what we are talking about.

Rocket on a String

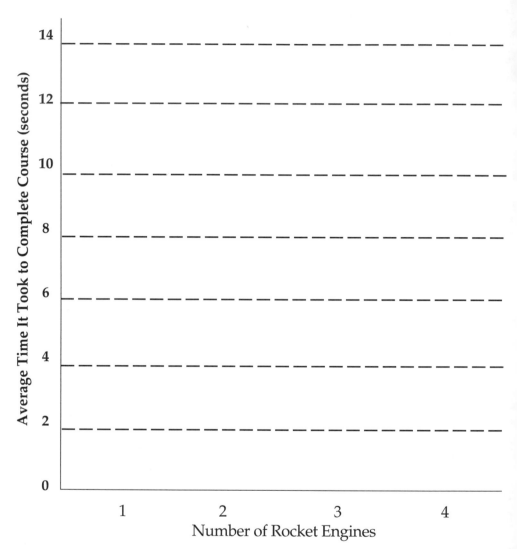

Extensions

62. Change the track that the balloon rocket travels down and use different materials. Try twine, fishing line, steel wire, and so forth.

63. Determine if the shape of the engine— round vs. oblong— makes a difference in the speed that a rocket travels.

64. See if your results replicate going uphill at a 45-degree angle.

Homemade Clinometers

The Experiment

A clinometer is device that is used to assist in calculating the height of an object. It uses a simple algebraic formula to determine that number once the base of the triangle and the tangent of the hypotenuse are known. It sounds a lot harder than it actually is.

Materials

1 Protractor
1 Index card
1 12" Piece of string
1 Washer
1 6" Piece of masking tape
1 Tangent table
1 Thick, drinking straw
1 Pencil
1 Water rocket launcher
1 Partner

Procedure

1. Lay the protractor along the edge of the index card as pictured in the cartoon on page 166. Using the pencil, trace the outline of the curve of the compass and then mark and label every 5 degrees from 90 back down to 0.

2. Tear the piece of tape into three 2-inch pieces and use 2 of them to fix the ends of the straw to the top edge of the index card. This is what you are going to use to sight or look at the bottle rocket as it travels up into the sky.

Homemade Clinometers

3. Tie one end of the string around the washer and the other end around the middle of the straw right above the 90-degree reading. Use the last piece of tape to fix the string in place so it won't move; and also tape the middle of the straw down so it won't move. Let the washer hang freely from the middle of the straw.

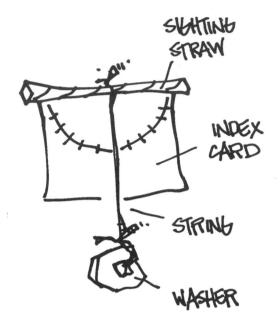

4. When you shot your water rocket up into the air, you didn't really know how high it went. By using the clinometer, an algebraic formula, and a couple of measurements, you can get close. This is the formula: The height of the object equals the tangent of angle a multiplied by the base of the triangle. Or, h= tan a•b. Here's how it works.

5. You measure a distance of 200 feet from the water-rocket launcher. This is the letter b identified on the next page; it is the base of the triangle. It always stays the same. While you are standing out in the field, 200 feet from your rocket, your partner pumps it full of air and it shoots up into the sky. All the while he or she is doing this, you are looking at the rocket through your straw.

6. When the rocket shoots, you follow it up into the sky, always sighting the rocket through the straw. This may take some practice. When the rocket reaches its peak and starts to come back down to earth, you hold still, keeping the straw pointed at the highest place the rocket was seen.

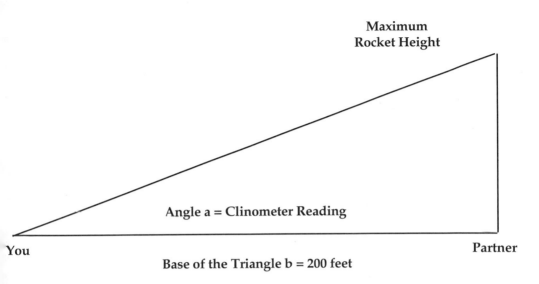

Maximum Rocket Height

Angle a = Clinometer Reading

You

Partner

Base of the Triangle b = 200 feet

7. Without moving the index card, look at the string. As it hangs down, it will cross one of the degree readings that you wrote on the card. Record that reading. Using the tangent table on the next page, determine *tan a* by finding the degree reading and then matching it to the equivalent tangent. Multiply the two numbers, 200 feet times the tangent reading, to determine the height that your rocket shot into the air.

For example, you are standing 200 feet from the rocket launcher, as always, and your partner shoots the water rocket into the air. You sight the rocket through the straw and follow it up into the sky. When it reaches the maximum height it is going to fly, you stop tilting the clinometer backward. Look at the reading. If it is 45 degrees, you look on the table and see that the tangent for 45 degrees is 1. To calculate the height you plug all of the numbers into the formula, like this:

Homemade Clinometers

$$h = 200 \text{ feet} \times 1.00$$
$$h = 200 \text{ feet}$$

So your rocket shot into the air. If the final angle was 25 degrees, it would be:

$$h = 200 \text{ feet} \times .466$$
$$h = 93.2 \text{ feet}$$

So your rocket shot into the air. If the final angle was 10 degrees, it would be:

$$h = 200 \text{ feet} \times .176$$
$$h = 35.2 \text{ feet}$$

Tangent Values

Angle	Tangent	Angle	Tangent
5	.087	50	1.192
10	.176	55	1.428
15	.268	60	1.732
20	.364	65	2.144
25	.466	70	2.747
30	.577	75	3.732
35	.700	80	5.671
40	.839	85	11.43
45	1.00	90	——

Water Rockets

The Experiment

This activity is going to give you an opportunity to build a launchpad using sprinkler pipe and then launch a 2-liter pop bottle hundreds of feet into the air. However, and we are required to warn you at this point, it won't be a cakewalk. As you work to achieve perfection in attaining these stratospheric heights, you will have to experiment with and determine the proper ratio of water to air to find the best propellant (the push to get the rocket off the launchpad). Likewise, you will have to address issues of vehicle stability and determine the most efficient pattern of fins and cones to aid your rocket in its journey into the galaxies and back down on top of the neighbor's doghouse. So, as they say in Houston, "Godspeed."

Materials

The first thing that you will need to do is put together your rocket launcher with all the PVC parts listed on page 170 and a little glue. All of these items can be found at the local hardware or sprinkler supply company. Using the pattern on page 170–171 as a guide, assemble all of the pieces. You will need to drill a half-inch-diameter hole in one of the end caps, you may want to enlist one of your folks or the neighbor with the cool drill press and too much extra time for assistance.

Remember that perfection rarely comes the first time out of the chute, so be patient. When you are done, you will have something that resembles a giant, slightly mutated, capital T.

Water Rockets

Materials

1   2-liter Pop bottle, preferably clean and empty
1   Bicycle pump, air tank, or air compressor
1   Bucket of water
1   Large, plastic, drinking cup to refill bottle
1   Bottle of PVC glue
1   Pair of PVC scissors
1   Drill with half-inch bit
1   Roll of masking tape
1   Tire valve
1   Pile of cardboard or poster paper

These PVC pieces are half-inch.
4   12" Pieces of pipe
1   8" Piece of pipe
1   4" Piece of pipe
1   3" Nipple
1   T joint (slip, slip, slip)
1   T joint (slip, slip, screw)
1   Coupling (slip, slip)
1   Elbow
3   End caps

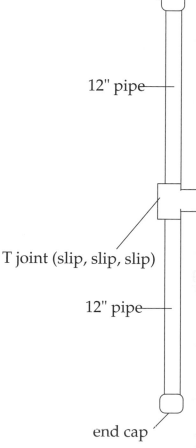

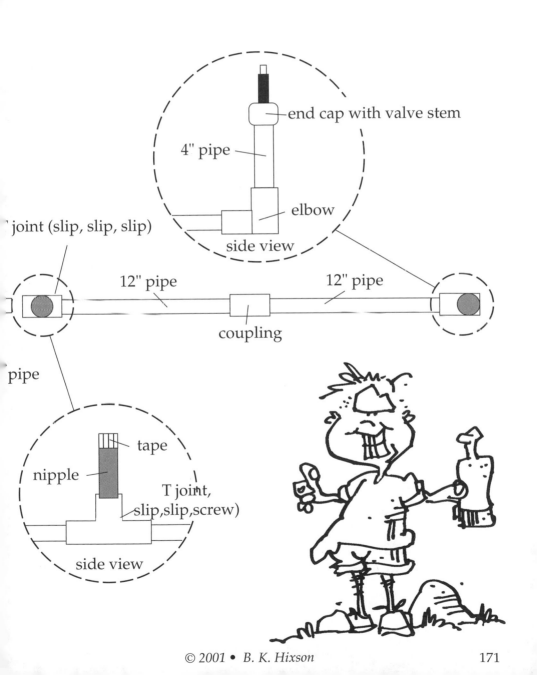

end cap with valve stem

4" pipe

elbow

side view

joint (slip, slip, slip)

12" pipe

12" pipe

coupling

pipe

tape

nipple

T joint,
slip,slip,screw)

side view

Water Rockets

Procedure

1. Once you have your launcher assembled, it is time to experiment with shooting the bottle into the air. To start with, fill the bottle half full with water and wiggle it on to the rocket launcher. If you look carefully at the illustration on page 171, there is a single wrap of masking tape around the nipple. The tape is there to create a tight seal, so that none of the water leaks out while you put air in. If the bottle is a little loose as you slide it over the nipple, you may need to add a second wrap to make the seal a little tighter. We are going to let you decide for yourself as you work through the different launches.

2. When you get the leaky water thing worked out, attach the pump and start to cram air into the bottle. You will be able to see the air gurgle up into your soon-to-be rocket. As the pressure inside the bottle increases, the rocket will be more and more susceptible to launch. Keep pumping and it will eventually shoot off the stand and up into the air. You don't have to do a thing except to keep pumping air into the bottle until the pressure gets too great to hold it on the stand anymore.

If you find that you pump and pump and simply cannot get the bottle to shoot, carefully walk up to the rocket and, laying on your stomach so you don't get a bottle up your nose, wiggle it upward. After the rocket launches, remove one of the wraps of tape so the seal isn't quite so tight.

3. Once you have launched your rocket a couple of times, you may notice that your rocket tumbled through the air, didn't quite produce a smooth and uniform flight path, and generally looked like a football tossed into a crosswind by a heavily sedated gorilla. To get the wobble out, you need to streamline your rocket—make it move through the air more smoothly. To do this you may want to add a nose cone and fins. No, actually, you will definitely want to add a nose cone and fins. That is what the cardboard or poster paper are for.

By now you have a pretty good idea what it takes to get the rocket off the launchpad. Now you have to improve the design to get it to go even higher. Try the following ideas and see what works for your rocket.

a. Design a nose cone to go on top of your rocket. Vary the steepness of the cone and change it from almost flat to very pointy. This may or may not make a lot of difference.

b. Experiment with placing fins on the side of the rocket. If you can figure out how to position the fins so that they create a spiral effect, science has shown that this adds stability and efficiency to the flight path . . . but how to get the rocket to do that?

4. Once you get the wobble out, it is time to experiment with different ratios of air to water to get the rocket to shoot higher. This will ultimately allow you to figure out the right proportion of water-to-air mixture to give your rocket the optimum boost. Use the data table on page 174 to record the data that you collect. As you look over the data table, you will see that there are three trials for each ratio. This will give you a better sample of information to work with. After you collect all three trial heights using your clinometer, average them out and then plot them on the data table on page 175.

By the way, your rocket has a capacity of 2 liters, which means that it can hold 2000 milliliters of water. Using either a beaker or graduated cylinder, fill and shoot your rocket with the mixtures listed in the data table and then record the heights reached by measuring with your clinometer.

Extensions

65. Of ourse there are all kinds of variations possible. The most common would be the size of the bottle.

Water Rockets

Mixture		Height Measurements		
Water (ml)	Air (ml)	Trial #1 Angle	Trial #2 Angle	Average Angle
0	2000			
500	1500			
750	1250			
1000	1000			
1250	750			
1500	500			
2000	0			

Calculate the average height for each ratio then plot it as a bar graph on the next page using colored pencils.

Height = distance from rocket x tangent of angle

Height for 0:2000 is _____ x _____ = _____ feet.

Height for 500:1500 is _____ x _____ = _____ feet.

Height for 750:1250 is _____ x _____ = _____ feet.

Height for 1000:1000 is _____ x _____ = _____ feet.

Height for 1250:750 is _____ x _____ = _____ feet.

Height for 1500:500 is _____ x _____ = _____ feet.

Height for 2000:0 is _____ x _____ = _____ feet.

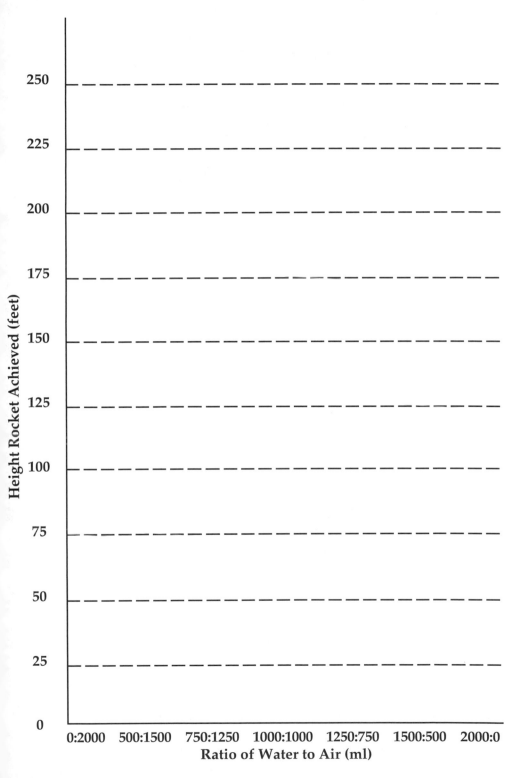

Science Fair Projects
•
A Step-by-Step Guide: From Idea to Presentation

Science Fair Projects

Ah, the impending science fair project—a good science fair project has the following five characteristics:

1. The student must come up with an *original* question.

2. That *original* question must be suited to an experiment in order to provide an answer.

3. The *original* idea is outlined with just one variable isolated.

4. The *original* experiment is performed and documented using the scientific method.

5. A presentation of the *original* idea in the form of a lab write-up and display board is completed.

Science Fair Projects

As simple as science fair versus science project sounds, it gets screwed up millions of times a year by sweet, unsuspecting students who are counseled by sweet, unknowing, and probably just as confused parents.

To give you a sense of contrast we have provided a list of legitimate science fair projects and then reports that do not qualify. We will also add some comments in italics that should help clarify why they do or do not qualify in the science fair project department.

Science Fair Projects

1. Temperature and the amount of time it takes mealworms to change to beetles.

Great start. We have chosen a single variable that is easy to measure: temperature. From this point forward the student can read, explore, and formulate an original question that is the foundation for the project.

A colleague of mine actually did a similar type of experiment for his master's degree. His topic: The rate of development of fly larva in cow poop as a function of temperature. No kidding. He found out that the warmer the temperature of the poop the faster the larva developed into flies.

2. The effect of different concentrations of soapy water on seed germination.

Again, wonderful. Measuring the concentration of soapy water. This leads naturally into original questions and a good project.

3. Crystal size and the amount of sugar in the solution.

This could lead into other factors such as exploring the temperature of the solution, the size of the solution container, and other variables that may affect crystal growth. Opens a lot of doors.

vs. Science Reports

4. Helicopter rotor size and the speed at which it falls.

Size also means surface area, which is very easy to measure. The student who did this not only found the mathematical threshold with relationship to air friction, but she had a ton of fun.

5. The ideal ratio of baking soda to vinegar to make a fire extinguisher.

Another great start. Easy to measure and track, leads to a logical question that can either be supported or refuted with the data.

Each of those topics *measures* one thing such as the amount of sugar, the concentration of soapy water, or the ideal size. If you start with an idea that allows you to measure something, then you can change it, ask questions, explore, and ultimately make a *prediction*, also called a *hypothesis*, and experiment to find out if you are correct. Here are some well-meaning but misguided entries:

Science Reports, <u>not Projects</u>
1. Dinosaurs!

OK, great. Everyone loves dinosaurs but where is the experiment? Did you find a new dinosaur? Is Jurassic Park alive and well, and we are headed there to breed, drug, or in some way test them? Probably not. This was a report on T. rex. Cool, but not a science fair project. And judging by the protest that this kid's mom put up when the kid didn't get his usual "A", it is a safe bet that she put a lot of time in and shared in the disappointment.

More Reports &

2. Our Friend the Sun

Another very large topic, no pun intended. This could be a great topic. Sunlight is fascinating. It can be split, polarized, reflected, refracted, measured, collected, converted. However, this poor kid simply chose to write about the size of the sun, regurgitating facts about its features, cycles, and other astrofacts while simultaneously offending the American Melanoma Survivors Society. Just kidding about that last part.

3. Smokers' Poll

A lot of folks think that they are headed in the right direction here. Again, it depends on how the kid attacks the idea. Are they going to single out race? Heredity? Shoe size? What exactly are they after here? The young lady who did this report chose to make it more of a psychology-studies effort than a scientific report. She wanted to know family income, if they fought with their parents, how much stress was on the job, and so on. All legitimate concerns but not placed in the right slot.

4. The Majestic Moose

If you went out and caught the moose, drugged it to see the side effects for disease control, or even mated it with an elk to determine if you could create an animal that would become the spokesanimal for the Alabama Dairy Farmers' Got Melk? promotion, that would be fine. But, another fact-filled report should be filed with the English teacher.

5. How Tadpoles Change into Frogs

Great start, but they forgot to finish the statement. We know how tadpoles change into frogs. What we don't know is how tadpoles change into frogs if they are in an altered environment, if they are hatched out of cycle, if they are stuck under the tire of an off-road vehicle blatantly driving through a protected wetland area. That's what we want to know. How tadpoles change into frogs, if, when, or under what measurable circumstances.

Now that we have beat the chicken squat out of this introduction, we are going to show you how to pick a topic that can be adapted to become a successful science fair project after one more thought.

One Final Comment

A Gentle Reminder

Quite often I discuss the scientific method with moms and dads, teachers and kids, and get the impression that, according to their understanding, there is one, and only one, scientific method. This is not necessarily true. There are lots of ways to investigate the world we live in and on.

Paleontologists dig up dead animals and plants but have no way to conduct experiments on them. They're dead. Albert Einstein, the most famous scientist of the last century and probably on everybody's starting five of all time, never did experiments. He was a theoretical physicist, which means that he came up with a hypothesis, skipped over collecting materials for things like black holes and space-time continuums, didn't experiment on anything or even collect data. He just went straight from hypothesis to conclusion, and he's still considered part of the scientific community. You'll probably follow the six steps we outline but keep an open mind.

HEY! GOOD NEWS AL, YOU'RE STILL IN THE CLUB.

Project Planner

This outline is designed to give you a specific set of time lines to follow as you develop your science fair project. Most teachers will give you 8 to 11 weeks notice for this kind of assignment. We are going to operate from the shorter time line with our suggested schedule, which means that the first thing you need to do is get a calendar.

A. The suggested time to be devoted to each item is listed in parentheses next to that item. Enter the date of the Science Fair and then, using the calendar, work backward entering dates.

B. As you complete each item, enter the date that you completed it in the column between the goal (due date) and project item.

Goal   *Completed*   *Project Item*

1. Generate a Hypothesis (2 weeks)

_____	_____	Review Idea Section, pp. 186–188
_____	_____	Try Several Experiments
_____	_____	Hypothesis Generated
_____	_____	Finished Hypothesis Submitted
_____	_____	Hypothesis Approved

2. Gather Background Information (1 week)

_____	_____	Concepts/Discoveries Written Up
_____	_____	Vocabulary/Glossary Completed
_____	_____	Famous Scientists in Field

& Time Line

Goal	Completed	Project Item

3. Design an Experiment (1 week)

Goal	Completed	Project Item
_____	_____	Procedure Written
_____	_____	Lab Safety Review Completed
_____	_____	Procedure Approved
_____	_____	Data Tables Prepared
_____	_____	Materials List Completed
_____	_____	Materials Acquired

4. Perform the Experiment (2 weeks)

_____	_____	Scheduled Lab Time

5. Collect and Record Experimental Data (part of 4)

_____	_____	Data Tables Completed
_____	_____	Graphs Completed
_____	_____	Other Data Collected and Prepared

6. Present Your Findings (2 weeks)

_____	_____	Rough Draft of Paper Completed
_____	_____	Proofreading Completed
_____	_____	Final Report Completed
_____	_____	Display Completed
_____	_____	Oral Report Outlined on Index Cards
_____	_____	Practice Presentation of Oral Report
_____	_____	Oral Report Presentation
_____	_____	Science Fair Setup
_____	_____	Show Time!

Scientific Method
• Step 1 •
The Hypothesis

The Hypothesis

A hypothesis is an educated guess. It is a statement of what you think will probably happen. It is also the most important part of your science fair project because it directs the entire process. It determines what you study, the materials you will need, and how the experiment will be designed, carried out, and evaluated. Needless to say, you need to put some thought into this part.

There are four steps to generating a hypothesis:

Step One • Pick a Topic
Preferably something that you are interested in studying. We would like to politely recommend that you take a peek

at physical science ideas (physics and chemistry) if you are a rookie and this is one of your first shots at a science fair project. These kinds of lab ideas allow you to repeat experiments quickly. There is a lot of data that can be collected, and there is a huge variety to choose from.

If you are having trouble finding an idea, all you have to do is pick up a compilation of science activities (like this one) and start thumbing through it. Go to the local library or head to a bookstore and you will find a wide and ever-changing selection to choose from. Find a topic that interests you and start reading. At some point an idea will catch your eye, and you will be off to the races.

Pick a Topic . . .

We hope you find an idea you like between the covers of this book. But we also realize that 1) there are more ideas about fluid dynamics than we have included in this book and 2) other kinds of presentations, or methods of writing labs may be just what you need to trigger a new idea or put a different spin on things. So, without further adieu, we introduce you to several additional titles that may be of help to you in developing a science fair project.

For Older Kids . . .

1. Science Project Ideas about Air. Written by Robert Gardner. ISBN 0-89490-838-3 Published by Enslow Publishers, Inc. 96 pages.

Twenty-seven lab activities are divided up into five chapters. This book is a very good resource, incorporating interesting facts, a historical perspective of some discoveries, and fun, easy-to-do, hands-on science experiments. It is a little less kid-friendly in its layout and titles than the other books we are suggesting. On the other side of the coin, the explanations are very thorough and the illustrations technically precise.

2. Best Ever Paper Airplanes. Written by Norman Schmidt. ISBN 1-895569-42-7 Published by Sterling Publishers. 96 pages.

If you love to build paper airplanes, this is a book that you definitely are going to want to get, along with the title that is mentioned next. The author has provided designs for 18 very cool airplane designs. Each design is named for a different kind of bird and shows a picture of the finished product. He then proceeds to give step-by-step instructions on how to build the airplane.

The preface to the book also includes tips on folding, launching, and maintaining your airplanes as well as a brief description of the principles of flight that provide the hours of entertainment that you will have playing with these ideas.

Find an Idea You Like

3. The Great International Paper Airplane Book. Written by Jarry Mander, George Dipple, and Howard Gossage. ISBN 0-671-21119-3 Published by Simon and Schuster. 128 pages.

Another great book with 20 more airplane designs for the flight enthusiast. *Scientific American* held a competition to find the best paper airplanes in the world. Categories included duration aloft, distance, and design; 1,128 paper airplanes were submitted to a panel of experts that included professors from UC Berkeley and Princeton as well as NASA and all of the major aerospace industries. You will have the 20 most successful and intriguing designs from the lot. Have fun.

For Younger Kids . . .

4. Air Science Tricks. Written by Peter Murray. ISBN 1-56766-082-7 Published by The Child's World, Inc. 32 pages.

Six hands-on labs written in a very entertaining fashion with great, colorful illustrations. Professor Solomon Snickerdoodle guides you through six hands-on labs that get you started on air.

5. Up in the Air. Written by Wendy Madgwick. ISBN 0-8172-5325-4 Published by Steck-Vaughn. 32 pages.

Another great book for younger kids. Twelve hands-on lab activities guide you through the basic ideas on air, air pressure, and how air behaves under different conditions.

6. Science with Air by Helen Edom and Moira Butterfield. Published by Usborne. 24 pages.

Lots of great illustrations accompany 25 hands-on lab activities that stretch across all of the same ideas covered in this book. The directions are clear and the text is easy to follow.

Develop an Original Idea

Step Two • Do the Lab

Choose a lab activity that looks interesting and try the experiment. Some kids make the mistake of thinking that all you have to do is find a lab in a book, repeat the lab, and you are on the gravy train with biscuit wheels. Your goal is to ask an ORIGINAL question, not repeat an experiment that has been done a bazillion times before.

As you do the lab, be thinking not only about the data you are collecting, but of ways you could adapt or change the experiment to find out new information. The point of the science fair project is to have you become an actual scientist and contribute a little bit of new knowledge to the world.

You know that they don't pay all of those engineers good money to sit around and repeat other people's lab work. The company wants new ideas so if you are able to generate and explore new ideas you become very valuable, not only to that company but to society. It is the question-askers that find cures for diseases, create new materials, figure out ways to make existing machines energy efficient, and change the way that we live. For the purpose of illustration, we are going to take a lab titled, "Prisms, Water Prisms." from another book, *Photon U*, and run it through the rest of the process. The lab uses a tub of water, an ordinary mirror, and light to create a prism that splits the light into the spectrum of a rainbow. Cool. Easy to do. Not expensive and open to all kinds of adaptations, including the four that we discuss on the next page.

Step Three • Bend, Fold, Spindle, & Mutilate Your Lab

Once you have picked out an experiment, ask if it is possible to do any of the following things to modify it into an original experiment. You want to try and change the experiment to make it more interesting and find out one new, small piece of information.

Heat it	Freeze it	Reverse it	Double it
Bend it	Invert it	Poison it	Dehydrate it
Drown it	Stretch it	Fold it	Ignite it
Split it	Irradiate it	Oxidize it	Reduce it
Chill it	Speed it up	Color it	Grease it
Expand it	Substitute it	Remove it	Slow it down

If you take a look at our examples, that's exactly what we did to the main idea. We took the list of 24 different things that you could do to an experiment—not nearly all of them by the way—and tried a couple of them out on the prism setup.

Double it: Get a second prism and see if you can continue to separate the colors farther by lining up a second prism in the rainbow of the first.

Reduce it: Figure out a way to gather up the colors that have been produced and mix them back together to produce white light again.

Reverse it: Experiment with moving the flashlight and paper closer to the mirror and farther away. Draw a picture and be able to predict what happens to the size and clarity of the rainbow image.

Substitute it: You can also create a rainbow on a sunny day using a garden hose with a fine-spray nozzle attached. Set the nozzle adjustment so that a fine mist is produced and move the mist around in the sunshine until you see the rainbow. This works better if the sun is lower in the sky; late afternoon is best.

Hypothesis Work Sheet

Step Three (Expanded) • Bend, Fold, Spindle Work Sheet

This work sheet will give you an opportunity to work through the process of creating an original idea.

A. Write down the lab idea that you want to mangle.

_____

_____

_____

_____

B. List the possible variables you could change in the lab.

    i. _____

    ii. _____

    iii. _____

    iv. _____

    v. _____

C'MON. HE SAID TO STRETCH IT.

C. Take one variable listed in section B and apply one of the 24 changes listed below to it. Write that change down and state your new lab idea in the space below. Do that with three more changes.

Heat it	Freeze it	Reverse it	Double it
Bend it	Invert it	Poison it	Dehydrate it
Drown it	Stretch it	Fold it	Ignite it
Split it	Irradiate it	Oxidize it	Reduce it
Chill it	Speed it up	Color it	Grease it
Expand it	Substitute it	Remove it	Slow it down

    i. _____

_____

_____

_____

ii. _____

_____

_____

_____

iii. _____

_____

_____

_____

iv. _____

STRETCHING!

_____

_____

_____

Step Four • Create an Original Idea— Your Hypothesis

Your hypothesis should be stated as an opinion. You've done the basic experiment, you've made observations, you're not stupid. Put two and two together and make a PREDICTION. Be sure that you are experimenting with just a single variable.

A. State your hypothesis in the space below. List the variable.

i. _____

_____

_____

_____

ii. Variable tested: _____

Sample Hypothesis Work Sheet

On the previous two pages is a work sheet that will help you develop your thoughts and a hypothesis. Here is sample of the finished product to help you understand how to use it.

A. Write down the lab idea that you want to mutilate.

A mirror is placed in a tub of water. A beam of light is focused through the water onto the mirror, producing a rainbow on the wall.

B. List the possible variables you could change in the lab.
   i. **Source of light**
   ii. **The liquid in the tub**
   iii. **The distance from flashlight to mirror**

C. Take one variable listed in section B and apply one of the 24 changes to it. Write that change down and state your new lab idea in the space below.

The shape of the beam of light can be controlled by making and placing cardboard filters over the end of the flashlight. Various shapes such as circles, squares, and slits will produce different quality rainbows.

D. State your hypothesis in the space below. List the variable. Be sure that when you write the hypothesis you are stating an idea and not asking a question.

Hypothesis: The narrower the beam of light the tighter, brighter, and more focused the reflected rainbow will appear.

Variable tested: **The opening on the filter**

Scientific Method
• Step 2 •
Gather Information

Gather Information

Read about your topic and find out what we already know. Check books, videos, the Internet, and movies, talk with experts in the field, and molest an encyclopedia or two. Gather as much information as you can before you begin planning your experiment.

In particular, there are several things that you will want to pay special attention to and that should accompany any good science fair project.

A. Major Scientific Concepts

Be sure that you research and explain the main idea(s) that is / are driving your experiment. It may be a law of physics or chemical rule or an explanation of an aspect of plant physiology.

B. Scientific Words

As you use scientific terms in your paper, you should also define them in the margins of the paper or in a glossary at the end of the report. You cannot assume that everyone knows about geothermal energy transmutation in sulfur-loving bacterium. Be prepared to define some new terms for them. . . and scrub your hands really well when you are done if that is your project.

C. Historical Perspective

When did we first learn about this idea, and who is responsible for getting us this far? You need to give a historical perspective with names, dates, countries, awards, and other recognition.

Building a Research Foundation

1. This sheet is designed to help you organize your thoughts and give you some ideas on where to look for information on your topic. When you prepare your lab report, you will want to include the background information outlined below.

A. *Major Scientific Concepts (Two is plenty.)*

   i. _____

_____

_____

_____

   ii. _____

_____

_____

_____

B. *Scientific Words (No more than 10)*

   i. _____

   ii. _____

   iii. _____

   iv. _____

   v. _____

   vi. _____

   vii. _____

   viii. _____

   ix. _____

   x. _____

C. *Historical Perspective*
   Add this as you find it.

2. There are several sources of information that are available to help you fill in the details from the previous page.

A. *Contemporary Print Resources*
   (Magazines, Newspapers, Journals)

      i. _____

      ii. _____

      iii. _____

      iv. _____

      v. _____

      vi. _____

B. *Other Print Resources*
   (Books, Encyclopedias, Dictionaries, Textbooks)

      i. _____

      ii. _____

      iii. _____

      iv. _____

      v. _____

      vi. _____

C. *Celluloid Resources*
   (Films, Filmstrips, Videos)

      i. _____

      ii. _____

      iii. _____

      iv. _____

      v. _____

      vi. _____

D. Electronic Resources:
   (*Internet Website Addresses,* DVDs, MP3s)

   i. _____

   ii. _____

   iii. _____

   iv. _____

   v. _____

   vi. _____

   vii. _____

   viii. _____

   ix. _____

   x. _____

E. Human Resources
   (*Scientists, Engineers, Professionals, Professors, Teachers*)

   i. _____

   ii. _____

   iii. _____

   iv. _____

   v. _____

   vi. _____

You may want to keep a record of all of your research and add it to the back of the report as an Appendix. Some teachers who are into volume think this is really cool. Others, like myself, find it a pain in the tuchus. No matter what you do, be sure to keep an accurate record of where you find data. If you quote from a report word for word, be sure to give proper credit with either a footnote or parenthetical reference, this is very important for credibility and accuracy. This is will keep you out of trouble with plagiarism (copying without giving credit).

Scientific Method
• Step 3 •
Design Your Experiment

Acquire Your Lab Materials

The purpose of this section is to help you plan your experiment. You'll make a map of where you are going, how you want to get there, and what you will take along.

List the materials you will need to complete your experiment in the table below. Be sure to list multiples if you will need more than one item. Many science materials double as household items in their spare time. Check around the house before you buy anything from a science supply company or hardware store. For your convenience, we have listed some suppliers on page 19 of this book.

Material	Qty.	Source	$
1.			
2.			
3.			
4.			
5.			
6.			
7.			
8.			
9.			
10.			
11.			
12.			

Total $_____

Outline Your Experiment

This sheet is designed to help you outline your experiment. If you need more space, make a copy of this page to finish your outline. When you are done with this sheet, review it with an adult, make any necessary changes, review safety concerns on the next page, prepare your data tables, gather your equipment, and start to experiment.

In the space below, list what you are going to do in the order you are going to do it.

i. _____

_____

_____

_____

ii. _____

_____

_____

_____

iii. _____

_____

_____

_____

iv. _____

_____

_____

_____

v. _____

_____

_____

_____

Evaluate Safety Concerns

We have included an overall safety section in the front of this book on pages 16–18, but there are some very specific questions you need to ask, and prepare for, depending on the needs of your experiment. If you find that you need to prepare for any of these safety concerns, place a check mark next to the letter.

_____ *A. Goggles & Eyewash Station*

If you are mixing chemicals or working with materials that might splinter or produce flying objects, goggles and an eyewash station or sink with running water should be available.

_____ *B. Ventilation*

If you are mixing chemicals that could produce fire, smoke, fumes, or obnoxious odors, you will need to use a vented hood or go outside and perform the experiment in the fresh air.

_____ *C. Fire Blanket or Fire Extinguisher*

If you are working with potentially combustible chemicals or electricity, a fire blanket and extinguisher nearby are a must.

_____ *D. Chemical Disposal*

If your experiment produces a poisonous chemical or there are chemical-filled tissues (as in dissected animals), you may need to make arrangements to dispose of the by-products from your lab.

_____ *E. Electricity*

If you are working with materials and developing an idea that uses electricity, make sure that the wires are in good repair, that the electrical demand does not exceed the capacity of the supply, and that your work area is grounded.

_____ *F. Emergency Phone Numbers*

Look up and record the following phone numbers for the Fire Department: _____ , Poison Control: _____ , and Hospital: _____. Post them in an easy-to-find location.

Prepare Data Tables

Finally, you will want to prepare your data tables and have them ready to go before you start your experiment. Each data table should be easy to understand and easy for you to use.

A good data table has a **title** that describes the information being collected, and it identifies the **variable** and the **unit** being collected on each data line. The variable is *what* you are measuring and the unit is *how* you are measuring it. They are usually written like this:

Variable (unit), or to give you some examples:

Time (seconds)
Distance (meters)
Electricity (volts)

An example of a well-prepared data table looks like the sample below. We've cut the data table into thirds because the book is too small to display the whole line.

Determining the Boiling Point of Compound X_1

Time (min.)	0	1	2	3	4	5	6
Temp. (°C)							

Time (min.)	7	8	9	10	11	12	13
Temp. (°C)							

Time (min.)	14	15	16	17	18	19	20
Temp. (°C)							

Scientific Method
• Step 4 •
Conduct the Experiment

Lab Time

It's time to get going. You've generated a hypothesis, collected the materials, written out the procedure, checked the safety issues, and prepared your data tables. Fire it up. Here's the short list of things to remember as you experiment.

_____ *A. Follow the Procedure, Record Any Changes*

Follow your own directions specifically as you wrote them. If you find the need to change the procedure once you are into the experiment, that's fine; it's part of the process. Make sure to keep detailed records of the changes. When you repeat the experiment a second or third time, follow the new directions exactly.

_____ *B. Observe Safety Rules*

It's easier to complete the lab activity if you are in the lab rather than the emergency room.

_____ *C. Record Data Immediately*

Collect temperatures, distances, voltages, revolutions, and any other variables and immediately record them into your data table. Do not think you will be able to remember them and fill everything in after the lab is completed.

_____ *D. Repeat the Experiment Several Times*

The more data that you collect, the better. It will give you a larger data base and your averages are more meaningful. As you do multiple experiments, be sure to identify each data set by date and time so you can separate them out.

_____ *E. Prepare for Extended Experiments*

Some experiments require days or weeks to complete, particularly those with plants and animals or the growing of crystals. Prepare a safe place for your materials so your experiment can continue undisturbed while you collect the data. Be sure you've allowed enough time for your due date.

Scientific Method
• Step 5 •
Collect and Display Data

Types of Graphs

This section will give you some ideas on how you can display the information you are going to collect as a graph. A graph is simply a picture of the data that you gathered portrayed in a manner that is quick and easy to reference. There are four kinds of graphs described on the next two pages. If you find you need a leg up in the graphing department, we have a book in the series called *Data Tables & Graphing*. It will guide you through the process.

Line and Bar Graphs

These are the most common kinds of graphs. The most consistent variable is plotted on the "x", or horizontal, axis and the more temperamental variable is plotted along the "y", or vertical, axis. Each data point on a line graph is recorded as a dot on the graph and then all of the dots are connected to form a picture of the data. A bar graph starts on the horizontal axis and moves up to the data line.

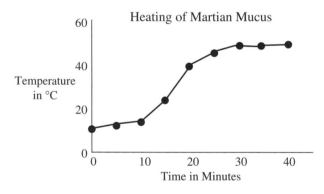

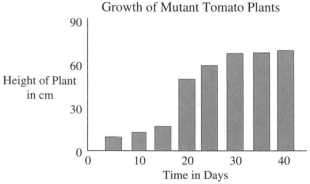

GravityWorks • B. K. Hixson

Best Fit Graphs

A best fit graph was created to show averages or trends rather than specific data points. The data that has been collected is plotted on a graph just as on a line graph, but instead of drawing a line from point to point to point, which sometimes is impossible anyway, you just free hand a line that hits "most of the data."

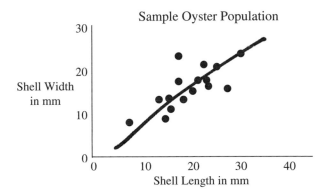

Pie Graphs

Pie graphs are used to show relationships between different groups. All of the data is totaled up and a percentage is determined for each group. The pie is then divided to show the relationship of one group to another.

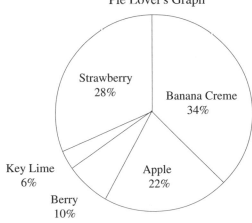

Other Kinds of Data

1. Written Notes & Observations

This is the age-old technique used by all scientists. Record your observations in a lab book. Written notes can be made quickly as the experiment is proceeding, and they can then be expounded upon later. Quite often notes made in the heat of an experiment are revisited during the evaluation portion of the process, and they can shed valuable light on how or why the experiment went the way it did.

2. Drawings

Quick sketches as well as fully developed drawings can be used as a way to report data for a science experiment. Be sure to title each drawing and, if possible, label what it is that you are looking at. Drawings that are actual size are best.

3. Photographs, Videotapes, and Audiotapes

Usually better than drawings, quicker, and more accurate, but you do have the added expense and time of developing the film. However, they can often capture images and details that are not usually seen by the naked eye.

4. The Experiment Itself

Some of the best data you can collect and present is the actual experiment itself. Nothing will speak more effectively for you than the plants you grew, the specimens you collected, or that big pile of tissue that was an armadillo you peeled from the tread of an 18-wheeler.

Scientific Method
• Step 6 •
Present Your Ideas

Oral Report Checklist

It is entirely possible that you will be asked to make an oral presentation to your classmates. This will give you an opportunity to explain what you did and how you did it. Quite often this presentation is part of your overall score, so if you do well, it will enhance your chances for one of the bigger awards.

To prepare for your oral report, your science fair presentation should include the following components:

Physical Display

_____a.   freestanding display board
             hypothesis
             data tables, graphs, photos, etc.
             abstract (short summary)
_____b.   actual lab setup (equipment)

Oral Report

_____a.   hypothesis or question
_____b.   background information
             concepts
             word definitions
             history or scientists
_____c.   experimental procedure
_____d.   data collected
             data tables
             graphs
             photos or drawings
_____e.   conclusions and findings
_____f.   ask for questions

Set the display board up next to you on the table. Transfer the essential information to index cards. Use the index cards for reference, but do not read from them. Speak in a clear voice, hold your head up, and make eye contact with your peers. Ask if there are any questions before you finish and sit down.

Written Report Checklist

Next up is the written report, also called your lab write-up. After you compile or sort the data you have collected during the experiment and evaluate the results, you will be able to come to a conclusion about your hypothesis. Remember, disproving an idea is as valuable as proving it.

This sheet is designed to help you write up your science fair project and present your data in an organized manner. This is a final checklist for you.

To prepare your write-up, your science fair report should include the following components:

_____ a.   binder
_____ b.   cover page, title, & your name
_____ c.   abstract (one paragraph summary)
_____ d.   table of contents with page numbers
_____ e.   hypothesis or question
_____ f.   background information
              concepts
              word definitions
              history or scientists
_____ g.   list of materials used
_____ h.   experimental procedure
              written description
              photo or drawing of setup
_____ i.   data collected
              data tables
              graphs
              photos or drawings
_____ j.   conclusions and findings
_____ k.   glossary of terms
_____ l.   references

Display Checklist

2. Prepare your display to accompany the report. A good display should include the following:

Freestanding Display

_____ a.   freestanding cardboard back
_____ b.   title of experiment
_____ c.   your name
_____ d.   hypothesis
_____ e.   findings of the experiment
_____ f.   photo or illustrations of equipment
_____ g.   data tables or graphs

Additional Display Items

_____ h.   a copy of the write-up
_____ i.   actual lab equipment setup

Glossary,
Index,
and
More Ideas

Glossary

Air Compression
Air is composed of a mixture of gases. When these gases are trapped in a container and the original volume is decreased by force, the air is said to be compressed or under pressure.

Air Contraction
Take the same mixture of gases and collect them into a container. That container is then closed, sealed, and cooled. As the molecules of gas cool, they possess less energy of motion. The less motion they have the less space they require. So when gases take up less space because they have been cooled, that is called contraction.

Air Evacuation
When heat or pressure causes air to leave a container, it is said to have been evacuated.

Air Expansion
As air is heated, the molecules of gas have increased energy. They bounce around more. The more they bounce around, the more space they require, so they spread out. This spreading out and taking up more room is called expanding.

Air Mass
This is typically a weather term. A large body of air that has common characteristics—temperature, pressure, humidity, and direction of flow—is considered a mass. It could cover a whole region of the country,

Airplanes
Big metal bird that flies in sky.

Air Pressure
At sea level we have approximately 100 miles of air stacked on top of us. This air is pushing down all the time creating pressure. At sea level it is about 14.7 pounds per square inch. The higher up you go in elevation, the less air is stacked on top of you, the less pressure is squishing you.

Angular Momentum

A force that is created when a gyroscope is spun. The mass of the spinning wheel produces a force perpendicular to the wheel. This force keeps the gyro spinning in place.

Atomizer

A tool that takes liquids and disperses them into millions of tiny droplets—very common way to spray perfume.

Bernoulli's Law

The behavior of fluids as they travel across a surface was first described by an Italian physicist named Bernoulli. He showed that the faster a fluid travels across a surface the less pressure it puts on that surface. That theory is the basis for modern flight.

Buoyancy

The ability of an object to float in a liquid.

Carbon Dioxide

A molecule composed of one carbon and two oxygen atoms. Most commonly found as a gas in our environment but at temperatures below 112 degree Fahrenheit it exists as a solid.

Clinometer

A tool that allows scientists to measure the height of an object or the height that an object travels. To measure these heights they must also know the distance from the base of the object and the angle that describes how high the object is or how high it flew. Then using a geometric table they can calculate the height.

Combustion

When something burns up, it combusts.

Glossary

Convection Currents
The movement of liquid or gases that is influenced by the amount of heat energy they possess. Cold air sinks as does cold water, and when they do, they displace the warmer bodies upward. As the warm air/water rises, it may cool and sink, displacing the water that is now warmer. This circular motion of cooling and heating is called a convection current.

Data
Information. It could be numbers, a picture, a recording of a voice or music, temperature, pitch, vibration, or any other quantifiable bit of information.

Data Table
A place where data is organized and tracked to produce a meaningful interpretation. Most data tables have variables and units to describe the data and how it was collected.

Density
A measurement that describes how tightly packed a material is. Density is figured out by dividing the mass of the object into the amount of space that it takes up. A common description would be grams per cubic centimeter or pounds per cubic foot. The more tightly packed the substance is, the higher the density.

Dry Ice
Solid carbon dioxide. Don't pop it into your mouth.

Equilibrium
A term used to describe when all of the forces acting on an object are equal. Everything is in balance. You haven't fallen off the bicycle, yet.

Friction
A force that opposes the movement of an object. Dive on the floor chasing a basketball, and then examine the lack of skin on your knees that was removed by friction. Friction can be created by solids, liquids, or gases.

Gravity

A downward force that is created by an object of very large mass. The Earth has a gravitational pull and the Moon, being quite a bit smaller, has one also, but it is only one-sixth the amount. This force pulls objects toward the center of the larger mass.

Gyro

A wheel that spins creating angular momentum.

Helicopter

A machine that flies by creating a downward force by pushing against the air mass under its spinning rotors. That downward force creates an opposite and equal reaction by the air mass, which pushes up on the rotors of the helicopter. This upward push causes the helicopter to rise. The rotor on the top of the helicopter is stabilized by a smaller rotor placed perpendicular to the top rotor. This second rotor is on the tail.

Mass

The amount of weight an object has regardless of gravitational attraction or pull.

Matter

Everything that takes up space regardless of the state that it is in currently is matter. It be a can solid, liquid, or gas and can be any temperature.

Oxygen

A pure substance that has a predictable and measurable melting point, freezing point, density, volume, and exerts a measurable amount of pressure. Usually a gas at room temperature and pressure unless it is combined with other atoms.

Rocket, balloon

A rocket powered by a balloon or balloons. These kinds of rockets typically have a very small payload capacity.

Glossary

Rocket, water
This is a rocket powered by expelling water under pressure from the bottom end of the container. The water and air leaving the back end of the rocket is the action, and the reaction is the movement of the rocket up and away from the launch stand.

Solar Balloon
A large balloon made of very thin, lightweight, dark material. The balloon absorbs the heat energy from the sun and radiates that heat to the air trapped inside. The air inside the balloon becomes significantly warmer than the air surrounding it and, being less dense, begins to rise.

Speed
A measurement that describes how fast an object is traveling. It is usually calculated as distance per time, for example: miles per hour, feet per second, etc.

Sublimation
Sublimation happens when a solid changes directly to a gas without passing through the liquid phase, or if a gas becomes a solid without passing through the liquid phase. In either case the liquid portion of the change is not invited to the party.

Tangent
Dude with a great tan. Just kidding. The tangent is a geometric measurement that allows a scientist to calculate the height of an object or the height that an object travels upward.

Vacuum
An absence of atmosphere. If the gases in a closed container are removed from that container completely and nothing is left, you have a vacuum. If there is some gas remaining inside the container, you have an area of low pressure unless that container is your brain, then we are back to the vacuum definition.

Vibrations

The regular movement of an object back and forth or side to side. This regular motion creates vibrations that can be detected with ears, eyes, and by touch. For you Beach Boys groupies and post-modern, hippie, wanna-bes, these are not the same as Good Vibrations or vibes.

Wing

A portion of a bird or airplane that, in cross-section, is longer across the top than across the bottom. This difference in length from front to back creates conditions where lift is created and the object can fly. Also, in the context of physics gone awry, wing means to injure slightly. For example, "Sorry about the rocket Pa, I know you think I dang near kilt ya, but really all I did was wing yer noggin a bit." Or something like that.

X-zylo

Half a soda can made out of very lightweight material. Completely worthless if you are trying to hold a soda, very entertaining if you can actually figure out how to throw the thing.

Index

Index

More Science Books

Catch a Wave
50 hands-on lab activities that sound off on the topic of noise, vibration, waves, the Doppler Effect and associated ideas.

Thermodynamic Thrills
50 hands-on lab activities that investigate heat via conduction, convection, radiation, specific heat, and temperature.

Relatively Albert
50 hands-on lab activities that explore the world of mechanics, forces, gravity, and Newton's three laws of motion.

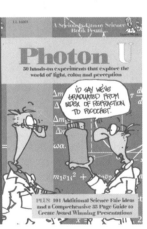

Photon U
50 hands-on lab activities from the world of light. Starts with the basic colors of the rainbow and works you way up to polarizing filters and UV light.

Electron Herding 101
50 hands-on lab activities that introduce static electricity, circuit electricity, and include a number of fun, and very easy-to-build projects.

Opposites Attract
50 hands-on lab activities that delve into the world of natural and man-made magnets as well as the characteristics of magnetic attraction.